CONVERS

CONVERSATIONS WITH

JACQUELINE

ROSE

ANTONY LERMAN

HENRIETTA MOORE AND STEPHEN FROSH

SUPRIYA CHAUDHURI AND AVEEK SEN

LONDON NEW YORK CALCUTTA

Seagull Books, 2018

This compilation © Seagull Books 2010

First published by Seagull Books in 2010

ISBN 978 0 8574 2 592 8

British Library Cataloguing-in-Publication Data
A catalogue record for this book is available from the British Library

Typeset by Seagull Books, Calcutta, India
Printed in India at Grafic Print, Calcutta, India

CONTENTS

ON BEING JEWISH

Ladies and Gentlemen, welcome to this session 'The Last
Resistance', and welcome in particular to Jacqueline Rose
and Antony Lerman, Director of the Institute for Jewish
Policy Research and author of numerous papers and arti-
cles on contemporary Jewish affairs, Middle East politics,
International Relations and anti-Semitism and racism.

ANTONY LERMAN (AL). Thank you very much for that kind
introduction and welcome from us also here. Good to see
so many people. I'm going to say a few words to begin
with about Jacqueline's book, *The Last Resistance*, and then
I'm going to launch into some questions.

3

The Last Resistance is a book of essays, articles and reviews that Jacqueline Rose has written over recent years, in which she reflects critically on the meaning of the journey the Jewish people have taken from the catastrophe of the Holocaust, from a devastated Europe to Palestine, to the present violence, death and destruction that we see in Gaza and Southern Israel on our TV screens. Her themes in this book are, among others, the consequences of Zionism, the nature of Jewishness, the ambiguous benefits of strongly felt identities, the impact of the enduring trauma of the Holocaust, themes that of course quite obviously closely interconnect. And yet, I think *The Last Resistance* is a difficult book to categorize.

Now, if you'd read those words that I've just said in a review you might think it a criticism but I'm certain that the author would take them as nothing less than accurate. The essays are mostly about people, people who can be labelled psychiatrist, philosopher, historian, novelist, political scientist, literary critic, but who in their work subvert their labels and actually defy categorization. Because what many of them offer on the book's themes is, and I'm quoting from something that Jacqueline writes in the book, 'no point of arrival, no resolution, no redemptive consolation', there's no quick fix—they're my words, not Jacqueline's.

In this book, I believe Jacqueline comes back to the subject of her last book which sparked such controversy, *The Question of Zion*, but she approaches it in a different way. In her own words, which may leave some feeling uncomfortable, she says 'My writing on Zionism is an attempt to enter into the terror and exultation out of which Zionism was born, to grasp the immense traumatic effectiveness of the Israeli nation-state. Traumatic not only for the Palestinians but for the Jews.' 'But,' she says, 'I have also wanted to revive the early Jewish voices who sounded a critique, uttered the warnings that have become all the more prescient today.' In her earlier book, these voices are Martin Buber, Hans Kohn, Hannah Arendt, Ahad Ha'am, some of whom called themselves Zionists. In this book although Arendt is a significant presence, the Jewish voices are Sigmund Freud, Ze'ev Jabotinsky, David Grossman, Marcel Liebman, Nadine Gordimer, Gillian Rose, and what links these, I would suggest, is not their reflections on Zionism so much as their reflections on their Jewishness and on questions of identity. 'Calling up these voices,' Jacqueline speaks of 'rebuilding the legacy of my own Jewish history.' By this, I wonder, does she mean fleshing out her Jewish identity? The journey through this book is not an easy one but that's deliberate. To reach the understanding she's seeking, she writes that it is necessary 'to be willing to lose our bearings and to enter, as all fiction requires, the strangest pathways of the mind.' And it's in fiction and in the minds of novelists, as well as in psychoanalysis, that she seeks insights into the fundamental questions she poses. How do we save people—the Jewish people—at one and the same time 'from the hatred of others and from themselves'? and in Israel's case, from the paradoxes of empowerment? She asks: 'Is there a way of wresting from Jewish history and thought a new polity, a new prayer to counter the worst of Israel's present-day dominion?'

Now whether you agree or not with the tenor of these questions, they are those of a politically engaged, public intellectual looking not just to understand but to seek to bring about change. Which brings me finally to the title of the book. If you are asking how to save people from themselves they are, I suppose, displaying a form of resistance, but are they resisting understanding, self-awareness, or do they simply resist, even though they may actually know the truth? But resistance also applies to those who oppose wrongdoing and oppression, so what makes some choose that path? So, I'll begin Jacqueline, by asking you I suppose, which of these is the last resistance, if either is, or is the last resistance something else, and why is this the organizing principle of the book?

JACQUELINE ROSE (JR). The title *The Last Resistance* I realize is in some ways misleading, and slightly provocative. I think when people hear the expression 'the last resistance', they immediately think of political protest, or of resistance to oppression or injustice, or the uprising of the underclass. Whereas I am also talking about resistance as obduracy, as something that gets fixed in the world and in the mind. The title emerges out of the tension between those two realities—on the one hand, I do believe there is something about the Middle Eastern conflict and about Zionism's definition of itself which is characterized by a peculiar and compelling intransigence, which makes it very, very difficult to shift the terms through which the conflict between Israel and Palestine is understood. On the other hand, I think one could fairly say two other things: one, that a lot of people in the world and in Israel itself know this, and are struggling with that reality and are resisting it—resisting, if you like, the resistance of obduracy; and two, and this is a psychoanalytic insight which is central to the way I think, any system that rigidifies itself too much, becomes too entrenched in its own conviction, is going to start showing the cracks in the wall, as it were. So, in a sense, the two concepts are utterly interdependent for me: there is an obduracy and it will fail, or there is a stubbornness and there will be an alternative. The two will always be running alongside each other in some profound and complicated way. I like to think that one of the things I am trying to do is disentangle the two.

One other thing, in reply to your question, and in a sense the most important one. I think, for many people, if you say the word 'resistance', you think of the resistance to Nazism—in that context, the word has a kind of sacred aura around it, which I totally understand and indeed respect. But one of the things I was doing in this book was tracking some of the different histories from the horrors of Europe in the middle of the twentieth century, to the creation of the Israeli nation-state. And noticing that that journey, which for some people is seen as absolutely automatic, as in, first horror, then redemption, is also for many of the participants in the first stage of that history, many of the survivors, something that they wanted to question. She only appears fleetingly in the book, but Hanna Levy-Hass, is crucial here. She was the mother of Amira Hass, the extraordinary Israeli campaigning journalist, and her remarkable document *Inside Belsen* [1946] is just about to be republished by the Other Press in New York. She did make the journey from Belsen to Israel but she became a very critical participant in the creation of the state. Or there is someone like Marcel Liebman, another sort of hero of the book, who chose not to make the journey but who lost his brother to Auschwitz, to the camps. So I was interested in the inevitability implied in one version of this history: from resistance to the Nazis and the awfulness of that moment and its moments of bravery, which are felt to be sacred and unanswerable, to what seems to me then the very risky next move, which is—*because* of that, *therefore* Israel, and, as often follows, therefore everything Israel does. I was very fascinated to see how many other stories you could write, just how many different ways there are of telling the story.

AL. Well, you cover a lot in that answer, and I want to come back to the question of histories, and particularly the path that you take from starting with the Holocaust and looking at the link between that and the present and how that is used. You use the word 'obduracy' and, in some ways, I think this is a very political book that is trying to find a way to break through that obduracy. For example, it is very interesting that you chose Jabotinsky to write about, but you draw attention to his radical self-questioning and ask if only other Israeli leaders had experienced the same thing, perhaps Israel might have been different. You also focus on David Grossman, who's a very important figure for you. You say: 'There's no other Israeli writer translated into English who goes so

far into the heart of the matter.' And then Nadine
Gordimer, Simone de Beauvoir. I wonder, is it your reading of the insights of these writers that has opened you
up to the path of political engagement with
Israel–Palestine, or was that engagement there and you
went to these writers to find some way of helping you take
that political path, or follow a political path that might
actually lead to some change?

JR. I'm not sure I can answer that question as one or the
other. It's a fascinating question which I've never asked
myself like that before, so I'm going to try and think on
my feet. My path to the question of Israel–Palestine came
through a very personal journey in fact—visiting in 1980
a sister who was living with the Bedouins in what was then
occupied Sinai, but also travelling to Tel Aviv and to
Jerusalem and having experiences which are slightly sur-
real in their momentousness. So for example, on the way
out on the plane I found myself sitting next to Dima
Habash, the niece of George Habash, who I'm sure you
know is the founder of the Popular Front for the
Liberation of Palestine. She said, 'Come to Ramallah'—
which was very easy to do in those days—'Come to
Ramallah and see what's happening.' And she asked me if
I was Jewish. When I said yes, she said, 'No doubt you
think the land belongs to you.' And I said, 'No, I think it

belongs to you.' I was surprised with the speed of my own reply. I think that was why she asked me to visit. Her mother refused to meet my sister and me because we were Jewish. She was running the United Nations Relief and Works Agency which was taking young women out of the refugee camps and training them to be dieticians, beauticians, dentist's assistants and sending them to Jordan, Lebanon and Saudi Arabia. Every six months, Israel would close the centre down and they would all disappear back into the camps, never to be seen again. It was a bit of a Sisyphean task if you like. When we were there—I'll never forget this—as we were approaching the centre, a number of these young women came rushing out to meet us in blue overalls, eyes ablaze with pleasure—we were foreigners, you know, people from outside come to see them. And they smiled and their teeth were rotten. It was like a political education in a split second, because there's no dentistry in the refugee camps. I had suddenly seen something which I had read about and I'd tried to educate myself about, but hadn't seen for myself. I think most people who become involved in this conflict one way or another have experiences a bit like this.

My reading then followed that, so in a sense this is answering your question. The reading came after. One day in Oxford, on my way to a lecture, I picked up a collection of essays by Amos Oz, *The Land of Israel* [1982], and I got very excited because there this was a dissident voice—at this stage I wasn't sufficiently educated, and had not been aware that there were such voices. From those two moments on, a process of self-education, which is still going on, began. And the people I read came to my aid, if you like. Hannah Arendt and Martin Buber and David Grossman—they are all people who, when I read them, I would think: 'Thank goodness there are people having these thoughts and writing these sentences!' Because they are helping me to think, and giving me a certain kind of foundation for a path which is of course a controversial one to take in relationship to the conflict. As indeed I realize pretty much any position you take in relationship to this conflict is, by the way. So, from that point on, I see it as a kind of nurturance by these writers. At a very basic level, it is immensely reassuring to discover that alongside the obduracy of a certain dominant rhetoric, a dominant state rhetoric and narrative in Israel, there are these counter-voices.

To refer to Jabotinsky in particular, it was extraordinary to read his short story, 'Tristan de Runha' of 1925, about a penal colony off South America, where the convicts' community ends up becoming more idealized and more positive than the civilized world. This is Jabotinsky

talking—it's not me—and he asks: 'Why?' Because there
was no iron on the island. Iron is what destroys people's
souls and gives Man the wrong belief that he can master
Nature and control the environment. This is almost exactly
the moment he is writing his famous essay 'The Iron Wall'
[1923], which, as I'm sure a number of you know from Avi
Shlaim's wonderful book *The Iron Wall* [2000], became a
foundational text for Israel's self-fashioning (one that
explains precisely the obduracy and obstructiveness of
Israel's relationship to the Palestinians), and which
argued that only if Israel becomes invincible will the
Palestinians, or the Arabs as they were called then, ever
be motivated to negotiate. Therefore the nation must be
superhumanly strong. Shlaim's argument is that
Jabotinsky's notion of what Israel needs to be has domi-
nated right-wing thinking in Israel to this day, has won
out over dissident voices and is in the ascendant as we
speak, as the events of the last few days in Gaza somewhat
confirm.[1] So it was wondrous to discover that Jabotinsky
was the thinker with the generosity and capacity to question himself and to put into his fiction a kind of pause for
thought, if you like, an ability to just stop and think: 'Hey,
wait a minute, maybe this isn't such a great idea!' and to
ask what might be its consequences, and, we can add
today, what have they already been. To say I was exhila-

rated by these writers would be another way of putting it. I'm not sure I've answered your question.

AL. I think you have. I want to come back to what you said just a moment ago, which is that, obviously, positions you've taken, the path that you've followed, have been controversial. One can't ignore the fact that your treatment of these subjects, your role for example in the founding of Independent Jewish Voices, has attracted much criticism, if not to say vitriol. You've been accused, for example, of eulogizing suicide bombers, and even a relatively sympathetic reviewer of this book said, and I quote, you 'romanticize the young men who desire the martyr's paradise'. So, since this is in the ether—well, it's more than in the ether, this kind of critique—how do you feel about it?

JR. Well, the idea that I eulogize suicide bombers is a source of great mystery to me. I tried to make it absolutely clear that I condemn suicide bombings and do not condone them in any way. I try to make a distinction between empathize—which is to try and imagine yourself in a situation where you would do things that, not being in that situation you can only condemn and hate; and sympathize—which is to sort of say 'great', which seems to me very, very different. I think it is very important to try and

14

understand what motivates people to do the things that are least comprehensible to the outsider. There is absolutely no eulogizing of suicide bombing anywhere, in anything I have ever written. I see that as a misreading. I do think it's quite interesting that in this debate, and this might be another way of responding to your question, misreadings are par for the course—you will be constantly misrepresented. To give you anther example, I've been accused of describing Israel as demonic. Well, I looked at that and I thought: 'This is strange—do I say that? I don't think I say that.' But, of course ,you can't remember everything you've ever said, so I started tracking back through to see whether I had. I found that it was actually a quote from David Grossman who said that we need to live in a world that is 'not ideal, not demonic'. It was a very sensitive and subtle remark about how idealization brings with it a risk of demonization which then implicates both the accuser and the accused, or more simply as I read it, how ideals can be dangerous. Apart from being a complex point, it was Grossman's expression, but that was good enough for this particular writer, who I think is the one you're quoting, for him to feel free to say that I described Israel as 'demonic'.[2] Amongst other things, *The Last Resistance* is a plea for careful reading, and a plea to be able to pause to think what people are trying to say, which is very, very hard in the cut and thrust of political life. But it is central to the world of teaching and writing, which is the world I'm part of.

AL. Obviously, it is important for people to read and to read carefully. And to understand and particularly interpret. But, as you know, we have to acknowledge that demonization goes on. What you feel and what others would feel is that there has been a great deal of demonization of people who want to dissent from the standard, orthodox view of these kinds of things, both in the Jewish world generally and in Israel. You say in your book: 'We are not allowed to acknowledge that the State [of Israel] intended to save the Jewish people has become the agent of policies which now place Jews in Israel and the Diaspora at risk, as well as producing intolerable lives for another people.' I wonder what you mean, though, when you say 'not allowed'—because this is a point of contention. There are people who've pointed out, for example when Independent Jewish Voices was launched, that Jewish intellectuals have never lacked space to say what they want to say, write what they want. So, perhaps in terms of careful reading, what are you saying when you say 'we are not allowed . . .'?

JR. That's a fair point, since of course you're allowed to acknowledge it, but at that moment I was referring specifically to Carmen Callil's book on the Nazi collaborator, Louis Darquier [*Bad Faith*, 2008], whose launch was cancelled because people took objection to one sentence where she expresses a link between her anguish at what happened to the Jews in Europe and the suffering the Jewish people are 'passing on' to the Palestinians. More generally, I think the point I was making is one that Mark Ellis has made very strongly in his writing. I don't know if some of you know his work—he's a Jewish theologian at Baylor University who has been a very strong critic of Israeli policies and actions; he is discussed in Sara Roy's wonderful new collection of essays, *Failing Peace* [2007], which came out last year, and which I know you, Tony, are familiar with. His argument is that it is very difficult, almost impossible, for Israel to see itself as the agent of violence, because the experience of victimhood has been so powerful in Jewish history that the idea becomes a form of anathema. He suggests that a sort of double-bind or impasse is at the heart of the way Israel sees itself which then becomes a legitimation for state violence, of the kind that we've been seeing in the last two days and many times before. It's not just Ellis who's said it. Shulamith Hareven, the Israeli writer—she is famous in Israel—who is sort of a heroine of the book, although she only makes a rather brief appearance, wrote an extraordinary article in the Eighties called 'Identity Victim' where she said that to see yourself as a victim is to give yourself a licence to 'commit any atrocity'. Now it's her expression—not mine. It was bolder than anything I think I might feel comfortable saying, but I thought it was a very powerful statement. One of the things I'm suggesting is that something has happened here to produce a kind of a lock in the system whereby, if you challenge the victim status of Israel, you are seen to be violating the ethical and psychological foundations of how Israel continues to see itself. 'Not allowed to acknowledge' really has a kind of psychoanalytic gloss to it, as in the idea of being in a certain state of denial—that there are certain things that you can't acknowledge because they would violate the entire mental system that has gone to work in order to make you feel secure about yourself. Although my argument is that the last thing it does is make you feel secure.

Let me just give you another example. For the first anniversary of Independent Jewish Voices, we had a meeting with Philippe Sands, the international human rights lawyer, and the Egyptian novelist Ahdaf Soueif. Sands made analogies between the way Israel is conducting itself in the occupied territories and the way Britain has been conducting itself since 7/7, in terms of what happens to a nation when it feels itself in danger and therefore mounts an argument against law in the name of national security. He gave quotes from British politicians who said effectively if not literally—'Sorry, the gloves are off! We now need a whole different way of thinking about things, because what's at stake is the security of the people. Therefore, we're going to change the law, or override the law.' He was making a provocative analogy between Britain post-7/7 and Israel today. But in the discussion it became very clear that in relationship to that analogy, or rather against it, Israel has to be seen as a special case because Israel was founded on the back of a concept of security—the very meaning of the nation is to provide security for a persecuted people. So the mindset he was describing has been there from the beginning. I think it's very, very difficult to do anything with it. That's again why the writers in this book, for me, are such wondrous thinkers, because they're all trying to do something with that mindset, including Grossman, Hareven, even Jabotinsky in his best moments. So 'not allowed to acknowledge' does not mean that you're not allowed to say what we're saying now—because, look, we're saying it, and you're here, which is great, although we'll see what happens later. Of course, we're allowed to say it, but there's a psychological cum political difficulty and I'm interested where those two things intersect.

AL. Right, but sorry to harp on at the question of demonization of dissent. I think that it's an important issue here because of the kind of reception that your work has got and that this book has got to some degree. I wonder whether you think that this is part of a kind of fracturing of Jewish discourse culture if I can put it that way, that this is more than just demonization of dissent, you know, the usual kind of argument between Jews that's gone on for centuries. It's something much, much deeper. I want to give you a sort of a personal example. What does it tell us when the *Jewish Chronicle* illustrates a recycled article criticizing Jewish Book Week for giving a platform to so-called 'Israel-bashers'—you; me; the ex-editor of *Haaretz*, David Landau; former Knesset speaker Avrum Burg—and illustrate this article with a cartoon—I don't know whether people saw this article, or whether they remember this cartoon—which clearly implies that we are all anti-Semites, because there are three people stamping, and eating, and setting fire to stars of David. Not the Israel flag, so the clear implication was of anti-Semitism. Do you think this is par for the course in our discourse culture, or do you think this is going too far?

JR. It's going too far. We could stop there but I think I slightly disagree with you. I don't think it implied anti-Semitism, I thought it implied anti-Jewishness—it was trying to imply that if you criticize Israel then you are detaching yourself from your Jewish legacy and you are in the process of destroying it. It is interesting to think whether those two critiques are the same, or which one is worse, in a sense. I felt the argument was that, if you criticize Israel, then you have no right in a sense to call yourself Jewish. In a way I think I take the suggestion that to criticize Israel is to destroy your own Jewish heritage more seriously—although the accusation of anti-Semitism I would also take extremely seriously—because it goes deeper, in a way, by attempting to disqualify the critic of Israel from her own history. It's going too far. I think it's scandalous. We took legal advice but, although the lawyer was appalled, there was nothing that could be done for complicated legal reasons.

On the other hand, I think it does show that those who have criticized Independent Jewish Voices, for claiming they don't get a platform, have missed the point, which is: not that one doesn't get a platform, it's what happens when one takes it. I think what is involved is a complex set of moves, aimed at discrediting any criticism of Israel whatsoever. There is a rather fine article which some of you will have read by Avi Shlaim in this week's *Jewish Chronicle* on this very topic in which he describes how the situation is deteriorating in this country, whereas until fairly recently we could pride ourselves on how distinct we were, say, from America.[3] I think we have to watch this space and watch it very carefully.

AL. I think you're right to bring this to the question of legacy, that the accusation levelled at you and at others, is that critics of Israel from within are detaching themselves from their Jewish legacy, and are beyond, or outside, the community. And yet, this book, in my view, as I said in the introduction, is very much about the question of Jewishness, and is a collection of writers and thinkers who are struggling with their sense of Jewishness, and for none of whom it is simple. You make that very clear in your analysis of these writers and the insights that you draw from them, because they're all in some sense at the edge, they all acknowledge their Jewishness but it's a very difficult relationship that they have with it. Yet you also say that this book is a celebration of Jewish thought. I wonder how you can hold those two things together—the fact that you write about the fractured nature of their relationship with their Jewishness and yet see it as a celebration of Jewish thought.

JR. Well, you are asking me some very difficult questions, don't you think? Which I appreciate. At this point, I

always appeal to Freud's remarkable statement in the
preface to the Hebrew edition of *Totem and Taboo* [1913].
In reply to someone who asks him to what extent he
defined himself as Jewish, he describes himself as igno-
rant of the language of holy writ, estranged from the religion of his forefathers, and unable to share the national
aspirations of his people. But then he adds that if he were
to be asked what is then left of his Jewishness, he would
reply: 'A very great deal and probably its very essence.' By
which he means that to be Jewish does not mean a com-
mitment to language, law, ethnicity or nationalism, or
even faith—it is something to do with a shared history
and heritage, a shared sense of belonging, something
communal, ancestral almost, and an attempt to work with
that towards a number of possible futures. Not just one.
So I would want to say that these writers, through their
very hesitancy, their engaged hesitancy with what it means
to be Jewish, are exquisitely Jewish in their thinking.

It was Edward Said who pointed to the remarkable
implications of Freud's analysis of Moses, in which he
argues that what's important about Moses is that he was
an Egyptian. And that there were in fact two Moses, and
that the people, the Jewish people, started by murdering
the first one. This is, to say the least, the counterintuitive
narrative of the founding of a people, I think you would

agree. The people are founded by a foreigner, there were two of them, and one of them was killed anyway. It must always be pointed out, of course, that this story has very little historical foundation whatsoever, as a number of Freud's stories. So then the question is: why does he want this story? In his brilliant essay *Freud and the Non-European*, Said argues that it is because Freud was trying to produce a version of national belonging which would not be grounded on monolithic singular identity, but would be plural and multiple and have a space at the very founding moment of its conception for the person who is going to be defined as the violent other of its self-constitution. That notion of a Jewishness that fractures identity, a Jewishness that therefore is aware of the fragility of identity, and can explore that with a strange, uncomfortable confidence is one that is immensely compelling, and which I would see as a celebration of Jewish thought. For some people these are the non-Jewish Jews, but by no means exclusively. One person I've been influenced by is David Hartman, who runs the Shalom Hartman Institute in Jerusalem. His book—*Israelis and the Jewish Tradition*—which I use in *The Question of Zion*, is a plea for the reconstitution of a Jewish spirituality, against the messianic Judaism of the settlement movement. So it's not an appeal for a secular state but an appeal for a state in which Jewishness would mean something else, and perhaps what it was meant to mean, distinct from the messianic sacralization of Jewish history and the land of Palestine. The question of what defines Jewishness is therefore up for discussion, to say the least, and I would really want to stress here that, for me, this is an ongoing part of my education. I don't claim to be an authority— it's something I want to go on learning about and these thinkers have helped me to do so.

AL. There's one in particular you write about who strikes me, the Belgian socialist Marxist, Marcel Liebman and you even wrote the introduction to a book of his, which was called *Being Jewish* or *Born Jewish*?

JR. It's called *Né Juif* in French. *Born Jewish* [2005]. There was a big discussion at Verso about how to translate the title.

AL. You quote from him—and I'm drawing out these quotes just to push you a little bit further on this question of Jewishness: 'Jewishness must find itself in the connections between peoples, whether in the Diaspora or in Palestine,' and then you say: 'Liebman's appeal is for a Jewishness not sealed behind walls of convictions, but open to the infinite possibilities of tomorrow.' Now I was struck by that, and it had resonances for me, but I

25

noticed that Anthony Julius, the lawyer, in an article he's written called 'Jewish Anti-Zionism Unravelled, the Morality of Vanity' which is on a website called z-word.com . . .

JR. Are you really publicizing this then!

AL. . . . calls this, because he has obviously read your essay on Liebman, 'a content-less Jewishness, of pure subjectivity'. So I just wonder how you respond to that?

JR. Well, I have had this article brought to my attention but so far I have chosen not to read it. I wonder how long I'll sustain that. But, in relation to Liebman, I don't understand what that means. He has the most extraordinary history. His 16-year-old brother was deported to Auschwitz. When he became a critic of Zionism, people would stand up at his talks and ask him how he could betray the deaths of his brother and of his people. And he would reply: 'On the contrary, I think of them very much.' It was because he remembered his brother that he was so frightened of a Jewishness that restricts itself to a national identity. It's as if Julius is saying that, unless you take on the national ideals of Jewish identity, there is no content to Judaism. With respect, I do think that's what he thinks. It's a position that can be debated, but it's one that I would really want to contest. There's a great deal left of Jewishness that is detached from nationalism. You only have to read the wonderful dissident Yeshayahu Leibowitz whose central argument was that the sacralization of the land and the state in the name of Jewishness was a form of idolatry, and therefore a destruction of Jewishness. Or Ahad Ha'am who in his own way thought the same thing. Or to be slightly more prosaic or grounded in today's political reality, when Rabbis For Human Rights take out full-page advertisements against the demolition of Palestinian homes, they appeal to Zion and the tradition of righteousness, and therefore to a tradition of Jewish ethics which they are setting against Israeli state policy. To imply that Liebman's Jewishness is void of content should be contested.

AL. Moving on, because we're going to open up to questions shortly, I just want to cover two other things although they're not really things that should be rushed at all. One of them is the question of the Holocaust which obviously figures large in the book. There is a chapter where you're responding to Judith Butler and discussing the contemporary implications of the Holocaust. One of the main points you make about the Holocaust is its instrumentalization, in (but not only in Israel) its use to justify, as you put it, the violence of state power. You quote Hannah Arendt from some notes she took for an article she was writing in 1963, that the notion that we can use our enemies for our own salvation has always been the 'original sin of Zionism'. And then—if I can have one last quote—you cite the historian, Idith Zertal, who recently published, with Akiva Eldar, a book called *The Lords of the Land* [2007] which is about the occupation. Zertal says: 'Zionism's work of mourning for the Jewish catastrophe still remains to be done.'[4] These are obviously very heavy statements and there's a lot implied in them, but I wonder if you could say what would need to be done to move, for example, towards this work of mourning.

JR. Well, some of you will know the wonderful book by Alexander and Margarete Mitscherlich called *The Inability to Mourn* [1975], written about Germany's relationship to what had happened in the Second World War. I think there is a very interesting question here which has been raised by people like Zertal, whose books have had a profound influence on me, and by Sidra Ezrahi, the Israeli literary critic, which is that once the Holocaust became part of a national identity—and a number of people locate this at the time of the Eichmann trial, when his capturing and public trial gave back a certain pride after what was felt to be the humiliation of what had happened in Europe—it became a collective project, and the grief for what had happened became re-silenced in a way. David Grossman tells *the* narrative of this in *See Under*

Love [1986]. When the Grandfather appears at the beginning of the novel, the family doesn't want to see him—he was meant to have died in the camps, but he's survived—and it's a kind of humiliation and makes the nightmare worse. The survivors were—and Zertal has done more than anybody to expose this—treated abysmally. They were called *sabonim* (soap), because they did not chime in with the notion of a renaissance of Jewishness out of the ashes of the Holocaust. But I think there's an important argument here: that, once that happened, once the trauma became part of a collective, national character-armour, if you like, which is, as I would want to stress again, more than understandable, then there's something about grief that goes. There's something about the language of politics and the hectoring of it—the argument is there in Judith Butler's *Precarious Life* [2004], for example—which feels at moments like a refusal to countenance any kind of psychic caution about feeling good about yourself.

It's understandable of course that a nation wants to feel positive about itself, but let's take an example closer to home—all the fuss about Prince Harry going to war. It's like an incantation: let's all feel good about Prince Harry. For me, this is a real example of the impoverishment of public discourse about war: let's feel great about the soldier prince. How about feeling depressed about war? It seems to me that would be a much better option. I think there is something here about an inability to mourn, which Israeli writers, like Zertal and again Hareven, have also commented on. Something has gone wrong here; though the memory is legitimate, there's still something that's not being allowed to be spoken. That would be an insight that I would want psychoanalysis to bring to politics—but how you do that I honestly have no idea.

AL. OK, one last question from me before we have some questions from the floor. There are two essays which for me stand out from the rest in this book, because of their very intensely personal tone. One is 'Continuing the dialogue—on Edward Said' which is actually addressed to him after he died, and the other is 'On Gillian Rose', on your sister who I had the privilege of knowing very briefly and spending a day with in Poland back in 1992. Anyway, Said died in 2003, your sister died in 1995. It seemed to me that the connection between the two essays in this book is clearly more than just personal. And I've picked out a couple of things you say about Said: 'The link between your literary and political thinking is key' and then you quote him 'the task of criticism is to be able to make distinctions, to produce differences, where at present there are none.' He said that very much in a political context. Then writing about Gillian, you say: 'She seeks to avoid at all costs a view of Midrash as a form of interpretative mobility beyond the reach of, and therefore safe from, the crises and destitution of political life.' It seems to me that both are saying that interpretive critical thinking is fundamental to and cannot be divorced from politics and from power. Which, I don't know, perhaps translates for you, personally, into a rationale for straddling the world of the literary academic and the world of political engagement.

JR. Well, yes . . .

AL. Is that something you'd agree with?

JR. I just want to agree.

AL. Thank you. OK, let's have questions. And only questions—no speeches, no statements, just questions.

QUESTION 1. Going back to the beginning of your talk, you mentioned that the Israeli occupation was the longest in history . . .

JR. Was one of the longest running.

QUESTION 1 [CONTD]. Well, what about Australia, North America, South America, New Zealand? I mean, aren't these occupations of a much, much different quality?—in that the local populations were completely obliterated, they had no rights. Putting Israel alongside them seems rather harsh.

JR. I was referring very specifically to the post-'67 occupation of the West Bank and Gaza, which has been defined under international law as an occupation. Your question raises the issue of how nations constitute themselves and would therefore lead us back to the question of 1948 and the question of the ethnic transfer of the Palestinians and to questions about the Native Americans. If you want to open that door, that's fine, but that wasn't what I was referring to—I was referring very specifically to post-'67.

QUESTION 2 [SABBY SAGALL]. I was very interested in your book *The Last Resistance* and in what you said in your talk just now, about the possible break or rupture between the kind of national identity represented by Israel and previous Jewish identity. As, for example, mentioned by Isaac Deutscher in *The Non-Jewish Jew* [1968]—of which figures like Freud, Marx, etc., are representatives—which also speaks of a kind of universalism of Jewish culture, of Jewish ethics, a radicalism that can identify with the suffering of the oppressed everywhere. But you seem to suggest in referring to a number of Israeli or Zionist writers that such a Jewish culture, such a Jewish ethic is still possible within the heart of the Zionist movement, or within Israel. I just wondered whether you could elaborate on that, and whether you think that squares with the analysis of Israel as a colonial settler state, which really has absorbed victimhood, as you said, to its very core.

JR. Well, David Grossman defines himself as a Zionist, and Uri Avnery, the founder Gush Shalom, defines himself as a Zionist, so the answer to your question has to be: yes, it is possible. But in response to what you've said, I'm thinking very specifically of Hareven who says at one point that there is an option here—one is to identify with the category of the victim, and the other one is instead to think of oneself as part of a more-than-two-thousand-year-old history of Jewish thinking and ethics, which centre on justice and the struggle for a more equitable world. It is a political choice—which identification you make. She was suggesting that is the choice that Zionism should make now. So I think it's an ongoing permanent challenge to Zionism today to modulate itself in this direction. That's why I do not define myself as an anti-Zionist, although lot of people would like to say that I am. I would say that I am a reader or critic of Zionism, but I'm not an anti-Zionist, because I can't be as long as I believe, and this is a psychoanalytic point, that no discourse ever is completely, totally closed. And certainly not this one. I think we probably disagree on this.

QUESTION 3. I'm trying to figure out your answer or solution to the Israeli–Palestine problem. You gave a hint of a of a bi-national state.

JR. Did I give a hint of a bi-national state?

QUESTION 3 [CONTD]. I thought you did, but from the Arab point of view, as far as I can see historically, Jews can live in Arab countries as a dominion, as a protected people, as second-class citizens. Isn't that really what would happen? I mean, what do you see as an answer to the problem, long term? I'm interested because I haven't heard this from you, ever.

JR. Ever? OK. The first thing I always say in this situation is it's not for me to produce an answer to the problem— the answer to the problem has to come from inside the conflict itself. I also know that's not good enough because I also believe it to be an international problem; that unless the international community does something and exerts a certain kind of pressure on Israel, this conflict is never going to be resolved. We know that if America changed its policy on the occupation, for example, overnight, if it started seriously withholding funds or making them conditional on a change in policy, the occupation would end. So, I think there is a real question of international accountability and responsibility here. On

the one-state/two-state solution—I don't think I can say
what I think should happen, but I can say what I think is
happening: that the viability of the two-state solution is
being destroyed as we speak, because of the expansion of
the settlements. That was why, for example, Shlaim
decided to defend a one-state solution at the Oxford
debate that was finally cancelled in October last year
when he and Ghada Karmi and Ilan Pappé withdrew
because Norman Finkelstein's permission to speak was
revoked. So, that is my position: the two-state solution
does not exist as a reality, therefore it looks like it's going
to be a one-state solution by default. But that will not be
the one-state solution that certain post-Zionists are advocat-
ing which is a state of all its citizens. Gideon Levy, the campaigning journalist for *Haaretz*, has said that it will be an
apartheid state because the non-Jewish citizens of that state
will be, systematically, second-class citizens, and there will
be no equality. So, at the moment the situation seems to
me frozen and heading for disaster. Ideally, yes, a state of
all its citizens. Daniel Gavron, the Israeli author, who
describes himself as 'mainstream, orthodox Labour
Zionist'—he was speaking here at the Jewish Book Week
earlier today, I unfortunately couldn't get to his discussion—I know that's what he believes in. In his book *The
Other Side of Despair* that came out in Israel in 2003, he

takes ancient Jewish history as his foundation and argues that in the ancient kingdom of David, Jews mixed with Jebusites, Canaanites, Hittites and Phoenecians. But, you know, I can't say what should happen, I can say what I think is happening.

QUESTION 4. I wonder if I could ask you how you feel that the existential nature of the Israeli struggle, the battle, affects the options that Israel really does have, and whether it perhaps doesn't justify certain actions, including violence, that would not under normal circumstances be acceptable?

JR. The existential nature of the threat is an expression used a great deal by Israeli state rhetoric itself to justify its actions. I would want to question that but not in an obvious or straightforward way. First of all, I want to question it in the sense that Israel is now the fourth, most powerful military nation in the world and the chances of it being wiped out seem to me to be very, very slim. We also know now that Iran has not been developing nuclear weapons, or that seems to be the American dossier's conclusion. However, even if that's true, and we cannot be sure, I think the existential fear is real, and that stems from the repetition of trauma through history. I think the question is how to square that circle—how to acknowledge the fear while not using it to legitimize what seem to me to be illegitimate policies and violence towards the Palestinians. For me, that is the problem, instead of saying, 'they're frightened, therefore their actions are justified.' I see that as a trap, the trap that a certain state rhetoric is caught in, and takes advantage of, and that's why I think we are where we are now.

QUESTION 5. And that's what prevents mourning?

JR. And that's what prevents mourning.

AL. OK, thank you all very much. Very interesting questions. I think we all appreciate Jacqueline's honesty and the depth of her understanding of these things, and, whether you agree with them or not, I think it's crucial that she's both listened to and read. And I do urge you to read this book which is full of insights and full of many things actually that we were not allowed—of course, we were allowed!—that we didn't have time to cover. So, please, let's thank Jacqueline.

JR. And can I thank Tony too, please.

ANTONY LERMAN is former director of the Institute for Jewish Policy Research. He is an Honorary Fellow at the Parkes Centre for Jewish–Non-Jewish Relations at Southampton University, and he writes for the *Guardian* and other publications.

Notes

1 In March 2008, Israel was intensifying its siege on Gaza.

2 The essay referred to is by Alvin Rosenfeld, 'Progressive Thought and The New Anti-Semitism' released by the American Jewish Committee in 2006, which became at the centre of controversy when the basis of a feature by Patricia Cohen in the *New York Times* in January 2007.

3 Avi Shlaim, 'Free Speech? Not For Critics of Israel?', *Jewish Chronicle* (29 February 2008). He is responding to the Oxford Union's withdrawal, under pressure, of an invitation to Norman Finkelstein to participate in a debate on the one-state/two-state solution.

4 Idith Zertal, *From Catastrophe to Power: Holocaust Survivors and the Emergence of Israel* (Chaim Watzman and Gila Svirsky trans.) (Berkeley, CA: University of California Press, 1998), p. 274.

PSYCHOANALYSIS AND THE POLIS

PSYCHOANALYSIS@LSE

A CONVERSATION WITH HENRIETTA MOORE AND STEPHEN FROSH
LONDON SCHOOL OF ECONOMICS, 22 JANUARY 2009

HENRIETTA MOORE (HM). Good evening. Welcome to this
event at Psychoanalysis@LSE. I want to begin by saying a
few words about Psychoanalysis@LSE just before I intro-
duce our two guests this evening. Psychoanalysis@LSE is
something that we have got going in the last two years
where we have brought together a number of important
thinkers to talk about what we think are the big issues of
the age. In other words, to talk about what's happening
in the relationship between individuals and collectivities
and the way in which sexual identities, family networks,
ideas about self and society are changing. Tonight, we are
going to take up some of those issues and talk about mat-

41

ters to do with nationalism, violence and the politics of hatred. But we are also going to address this wonderful new book by Professor Jacqueline Rose, *The Last Resistance*.

Professor Rose is Professor of English at Queen Mary University of London, and is a very well-known scholar for her work on the relationship between psychoanalysis, feminism and literature. She is, I have no hesitation in saying, one of the few genuine public intellectuals in the UK at the moment and you will read her work regularly in the *London Review of Books* and in other places where they take thinking seriously, and it is a very great pleasure to welcome her here to the LSE.

Professor Stephen Frosh is Professor of Psychology, he is also Pro-Vice Master at Birkbeck and has written extensively on the relationship between psychoanalysis and social thought, on psychoanalysis and politics. He has also written, as Professor Rose has, on issues to do with Zionism and with hatred. So we're going to begin the evening by Stephen introducing Jacqueline's book for you and then we are going to enter into a conversation among the three of us about what we think is important.

STEPHEN FROSH (SF). Thank you, Henrietta. I was explaining to Jacqueline before that I read the book for a second time, preparing for this evening, and was really moved by it and decided I would write some notes for myself and ended up writing a kind of letter to Jacqueline. And so what I'm going to do is actually read this letter as the beginning piece of the conversation.

Dear Jacqueline, I think this is a particularly important book in a long series of significant works by you. Arising out of a lecture originally given here at the LSE which provides the title and also one of the abiding themes of the book, it seems to me to draw together a number of threads that have characterized your work and to create something that is especially moving and difficult—what you refer to as 'the interval of reflection', that is one of your objects of study. So, before we start the conversation, I wanted to highlight a few of these threads, both to orient people who might not yet have read the book and to open up some areas that we might discuss. Like most strong work, *The Last Resistance* is a deeply engaged piece of writing, with a constant movement across psychoanalysis, politics and the personal. The personal is drawn on to explore political and intellectual concerns, for instance your memorializing pieces on two people whose lives and work were deeply entwined with your own—Edward Said and your own sister, Gillian. And, conversely, your political and literary work is fuelled by deeply felt ethical and personal concerns, as in your probing of Zionism and your teaching, referred to a few times in the book, on Israeli, Palestinian and South African Literature. This is rooted in a mode of Jewish identity politics that is searching and deliberately equivocal, in the sense of being open and fractured, rather than, as perhaps is characteristic of the nationalisms that you explore, being fixed and certain. Your openness is, I think, an intentional strategy for questioning and disturbing, for insisting on what you refer to as 'an interval of reflection'. This interval is technically between impulse and action as the moment in which identification and thoughtfulness can occur, in which it becomes possible to imagine a position outside your own. On the whole, the identification you're looking for is with another person's pain. In Said's remarkable phrase about Israelis and Palestinians, which you quote and worry over, he says: 'We cannot co-exist as two communities of detached and uncommunicatingly separate suffering . . . there is suffering and injustice enough for everyone.' I take this to be one of the epigraphs of the book, that an interval for reflection is not only the space between impulse and action but also one of the conditions for being human, or perhaps a grounding of human ethics; 'there is suffering an injustice enough for everyone,' writes Said. And you

44

say elsewhere that the important thing is to enter into the pain of the other. 'Passing on pain' you write 'would be the political opposite of entering the pain of the other.' I wonder if you agree that a major theme running through the book is how difficult it is to do this entering into, how pain gets acted upon, acted out upon, to and through the other, how it routinely gets passed on, and how unremittingly, in your view, this can be seen in your main political concern—what's being done to the Palestinians. I want to stay for a moment with this issue of the interval of reflection. Much of this book is an investigation of a certain kind of committed fiction-writing. Indeed, the two pillars of the book are fiction and psychoanalysis, each used in its own way to pursue something which might in other places be called 'truth', but is here presented as a kind of rigorous and relentless thinking through. In the case of fiction, what's important is its power to produce troubling identifications that overcome one of the types of resistance with which you deal—the resistance of the mind to understanding what might be the position or experience, or possibility, of the repudiated other. In the context, for instance, of Arnold Zweig's surprised, uneasy and profoundly disturbing fictional reconstruction of a murderous moment in Zionist history, you identify as one of your preoccupations the power of fiction to make reader, as well as writer, enter pathways that they have never in their wildest dreams intended to tread. But why put ourselves to such trouble? Why allow fiction to trouble us so, as it does in much of the work that you quote from J. M. Coetzee to *Suite Francaise* [Irène Némirovsky, 2004]? You write, taking the offensive: 'But why, I would ask, if we need to understand the worst as well as the best of history, would you want to stop the mind from running away with itself?'

Literary analysis and psychoanalysis are brought together here in what is an exquisitely ethical move. To avoid passing on pain, we have an obligation to let the mind run away with itself, to think things through to the end, even if this means being the subject of opprobrium because, for example, one tries to understand suicide bombers. This is not the same I think, in your writing, as a liberal position that everyone can and should be understood, that there are always identifiable reasons, even classic psychoanalytic reasons, for actions. You know that sometimes burrowing into the psyche of the enemy is a form of evasive action designed to blind you to the responsibility for their dilemma that is staring you in the face. The difficulty of this situation is immense, the interval of reflection doubles back on itself and ethics become something that can be found only in the process of pursuing thought to its end, of doubling and redoubling its painful reflexivity. You say: 'We need to find a language that will allow us to recognize why, in a world of rampant inequality and injustice, people are driven to do things that we hate.' But what might that language be if it's not to be one of self-effacement, or blame, or liberal empathy?

Psychoanalysis is right at the centre of this interval. Like fiction, what it promotes is not in any meaningful sense self-knowledge but a kind of un-self-imaginative capacity. Freud, you know, did not believe in the ideals of the mass. 'In reality,' you quote him, 'our fellow citizens have not sunk so low as we feared, because they have never risen as high as we believed.' Psychoanalysis in this book is not treated as a technical, therapeutic discipline, though the technicalities of resistance and displacement have their resonance; it is, rather, the possibilities of phantasy that you emphasize. With phantasy here being, in your words from a previous book, 'thicker than water'. The thickness of phantasy in *The Last Resistance* refers I think to the specifically Freudian, though perhaps also Jewish, deployment of a self-lacerating rationalism. There is nothing so unrelenting as psychoanalytic thought when it is turned on the motives of human action, one's own and that of the nation, especially when what it finds is that the supposed evil out there is found within—in the

subject, in the mass, in the social order that passes it on.
Hence the doubleness of resistance, at its purest and
apparently most political, is resistance to oppression, then
is resistance to the other, then also resistance to knowledge, now a regressive and defensive act. In this hard
place in which there is so little space to turn, how can the
former mode of resistance overcome the latter? That is,
what are the political possibilities of resistance understood in its full psychoanalytic doubleness?

And finally, a note on the Jewish element in this, the
full reference to the interval of reflection is in your
description of the book as 'a celebration of Jewish
thought, as it lays claim to the interval of reflection'. And
most of the writers with whom you concern yourself were
Jewish, several of them, including your sister, writing on
Jewish issues including Zionism. What exactly, I wonder
here, makes this Jewish thought? And do you think the
interval of reflection is intrinsic to it? And if so, is there a
kind of betrayal or loss at the moment in which the interval is denied? The book seems to me to move between
particularism and universalism, with the latter your pref-
erence. You note apparently with approval how Marcel
Liebman did dedicate his memoir to Jews and non-Jews
fighting against Nazism. But the former, the particularism, is implicit in the reference to Jewish thought and to

your own concentration on the topics you have chosen. Or is thought only truly Jewish when it's ethically universalist? And if so, is that to demand of it the impossible?

JACQUELINE ROSE (JR). Well, I think we can all go home now. Thank you, genuinely, for that. It's going to be hard to proceed, picking out the difficult points for discussion, so we're really going to be relying on you as well as on Henrietta. The first thing I want to say is how pleased I am to be here. It really matters to me that I gave the opening essay of the book here as a lecture, not just in this room but here at the LSE, at a time when I think the programme for the place of psychoanalysis at the LSE was really just in its very opening stages. It was a wonderful conference called 'Flesh and Blood; Psychoanalysis, Politics and Resistance' where I did talk about a novel by the writer Arnold Zweig that was central to his communication and correspondence with Freud. *De Vriendt Goes Home* [1933] was a very strange novel about a political murder in Israel, of a Zionist. Originally, it had been thought that this man had been assassinated because he was a homosexual, by Arabs, but it turned out that he had been assassinated by right-wing Zionists because he had become a critic of Zionism. Zweig writes to Freud that this discovery could have spelled the end of the plan; instead, the 'flaw' in the original idea became the basis of his creativity in writing the book. It was part of his need to acknowledge that violence and mayhem could be at the heart of a liberatory, self-emancipatory, movement of national self-determination which is how Zionism defines itself. So it was a psychoanalytic move of exposing violence where it should not have been. The reason for stressing this is that it was very important to me to talk about fiction here at the LSE, because it is my understanding that at the LSE, which is one of the institutions in London that I respect most for its range, the people it has involved in its work and the possibilities of teaching, fiction plays an even smaller role than psychoanalysis. What I would like is for fiction to be seen as central to the way in which we conceive of political and national identities, and as a means for understanding how they can be more interesting, more shifting, less rigid, than the dominant forms of national identification imposed on, or taken up, by people in their political lives.

HM. Let me start with a small question—what I'm interested in is the multiple ways in which we are national subjects. So the question is: is literature the only space for us in which we can see the multiply constituted subject negotiating the terrain of self and of relation with others? I mean, students here, for example, may not have been reading much literature but they probably are going to the cinema. So do you think that the argument you make for literature could be as persuasively made for the performing arts, for music, for cinema?

JR. Well this is a very complex question. I certainly think it can be made for the performing arts and for cinema but up to a point, and I'll say where I think that point ends in a minute. In relation to the arts, just recently I've been looking at the work of Esther Shalev-Gerz, the Lithuanian born artist who lived in Israel for twenty-five years and who now lives in Paris. She became famous for the 'Monument Against Fascism' which she created with Jochen Gerz in Harburg in 1986. She has been working for a number of years on testimony, in relation to the Holocaust but also in relation to contemporary public spaces, but she does it in a very strange way by having, for example, multiple representations of different voices all punctuating and pausing at the same time, with close-ups of their bodies and faces. So that you really have to get close to them in ways you don't get close to people unless you're going to hit them or have sex with them. It's very disorienting about the relationship between an observer and a body, and very disorienting about the relationship between voice, testimony, memory and history. And it's quite brilliant—an attempt to embody or enact, if you will, a modern version of the diverse speech which for Hannah Arendt constituted the *polis*. For example, she does projects involving asking people, in Aubervilliers outside Paris, in West Bromwich most recently, often immigrants, to tell their stories, her question always being: 'What story would you like to tell?' It makes you hyperconscious of what it means to tell a story, and because the stories are placed—contrapuntally we might say—in relationship to each other and to you as viewer, that divests them of any naivety. It's not simply 'this is who I am', something breaks up under the pressure of the forms of representation she brings to bear on them. So certainly you can do it in other forms.

In relation to cinema, it depends on which cinema we're talking about. I'm always reminded of Bertolt Brecht's 'fundamental reproach' against cinema—a term from his Work Journal on which, Ben Brewster, the film critic and editor of *Screen* magazine, wrote an article in the Seventies—which was that the spectator always sees what the camera is showing her or him. You are in a sense seized by the control of the camera eye. And you can't stop the film, you can't go back and read that section again—you can if you watch it on a Steenbeck or in an editing studio, but, until the advent of DVD, etc., that was an unusual and slightly perverse activity—but you don't have what you have with literature, which is when you're reading it, you pause, you forget, you go back, you pick it up, you put it down. There is something about a film, even in the home, to do with its drivenness which is part of the viewing experience itself. For that reason, I think it's very hard in cinema to produce the level of complexity of identification that I think is possible in fiction, which is not to say that there isn't a whole tradition of avant-garde and experimental film which aims precisely to do that.

There is also something, I think, about language. Jacques Lacan once said the only people who could really understand psychoanalysis were literature students, and people who wrote literature, because they are not fazed by the fact that one word can mean more than one thing at the same time, and might contradict itself. Indeed, they take great pleasure—that's probably why we become literary students—in the fact that a word can carry two completely contrary meanings, and in holding that ambiguity or tension in place. Whereas, if you're in one of the positive sciences, the instability of language, the way it floats over and away from meaning, is a problem that has to be bypassed or ignored. However, Henrietta, you write about multiple identities as part of anthropology, so in a sense you should be answering your question.

HM. Well, that's maybe why I asked it.

SF. Can I ask something related? If that's the specificity of literature, what do you think is the specificity of psychoanalysis in this?

JR. Well, the specificity of psychoanalysis is that it believes we are spoken by the unconscious, and that we are internally divided, unstable, subjects, and that there are possibilities in our unconscious minds that we would prefer not even, sometimes, to dream of. This does relate to your work, Henrietta, because in your most recent book *The Subject of Anthropology*, when you are talking about a possible link between the psychoanalytic and the anthropological subject, you have a phrase which I felt you wrote for me where you say 'you have to see that subjects both identify with and resist subject-positions.'[1] I would never use, by the way, the expression subject-positions because I feel if you are a subject you are never in position—I see that expression as an oxymoron. But 'identify with and resist' I love, because I think it is the specificity of psychoanalysis that something about your identity is always on the lookout for other possibilities, and always radically distrustful of its greatest points of certainty. So for example, Moustapha Safouan, the Paris-based Egyptian psychoanalyst whose book on Lacan and training I had the privilege of translating some years ago, states that to the extent that someone asserts that they are heterosexual at the level of their conscious life, you can be sure that the opposite is being said in the unconscious. There is a radical un-fit between what we assert in language and what is being unravelled in the unconscious and this can strike at our most passionately cherished forms of social identity and belonging.

SF. Yet, as we know, that is a particular kind of psychoanalysis, which in many of its manifestations takes precisely the kind of normative, conservative mode of thinking as well as practice that the line you've just taken opposes, just as I suppose you could say fiction can do that too. You know, fiction can ameliorate and take you away from thinking things through. You are a very sophisticated writer about psychoanalysis and know an enormous amount of psychoanalysis in its different forms but, in the book, when looking for the kind of disruptive psychoanalysis that's needed for the argument about resistance, you turn only to Freud—there's one or two references to Winnicott, maybe one to Bollas—he is the recurring psychoanalyst. There's virtually no post-Freudian thought at all. My query is: is there an idealization of psychoanalysis that takes place among some of us? I share a lot of it, you know. It's not a criticism, but a question about whether such an idealization becomes necessary if you want to hold on to psychoanalysis as a potentially critical practice in this political sphere?

JR. You raise a very important issue. In the book I translated by Moustapha Safouan—*Jacques Lacan and The Question of the Training of Psychoanalysts* [2000]—he argues that there's been a real dilemma in psychoanalytic training and the creation of analysts, where, after a complex historical path, the version of training that won out in the international psychoanalytic association was a very rigid conception. For Lacan, that version of training had stopped certain key questions being asked about how you transmit knowledge, since the central psychoanalytic tenet, through Oedipus, is that you can't simply transmit anything because we're haunted, rebellious subjects, no more so than in the passage from father to son. The idea that you become like your analyst, or move into their place, as you do in a way by receiving their legacy and taking up an accredited position in their institution, is fraught with anxiety, a kind of nonsense. There's a founding disjunction for which it is very hard to produce a set of training rules or procedures. This is a very difficult question about what it means to become a psychoanalyst and what forms of identification with certain schools of thought that training imposes on you. Can you become an analyst without identifying with your analyst's own school, indeed in a sense with her or his analysis, even though, as a crux or problem, that is unlikely to be spoken?

However, having said that, it also depends on how individual analysts read the corpus. In this book, you're right, I talk about Freud much more than I talk about anybody else. But I have written about and indeed translated Lacan, still radically important for me. And if you take someone like Melanie Klein, who could be said to represent a type of orthodoxy, there are ways of reading which go against the dominant narrative of what any one analyst may have been allowed, partly institutionally, to become. For instance, there is a way of reading Klein in terms of the passage from the paranoid/schizoid position to the depressive position as involving a certain genital normativity. There's no question that you can read her like that, and that, at moments, she invites such a reading. But there are other ways of reading her—I know that someone like Daniel Pick, who teaches history at Birkbeck and is also a practising psychoanalyst, will insist on this— which is to say that none of those positions are ever acquired, nor can they ever be assumed to be, and that it is not the task of analysis to convince you that they have acquired a stable identity. We were having a discussion last week at the graduate forum—Psychoanalytic Thought, History and Political Life—which we organize together where we precisely try and engage these questions of what psychoanalysis has to say about politics and what it says about itself. His opinion is that there's a normative reading of Klein and there's one which is, not radical—he's not arguing for it as radical—but which knows the tentative nature of even its most developmental and normative moments. So I think it's very hard to generalize and I'm surprised you generalize as confidently as you do, Stephen, in saying that most psychoanalytic practices become normative. I would want you to say more on who you're talking about, which is not to ignore institutional prejudice against homosexuality, to take the most obvious example, or prejudice inscribed in the classic texts. Of course that can be, and crucially has been, identified. But I would say that you have to see who's writing in what way, and what's being done with what they've written, and then ask what it means to create an institutional tradition and a legacy out of writing. That's when I think the problems begin and things get very tricky.

HM. OK, so could we go back for a moment then to the question of the relationship between psychoanalysis and politics, and what might be in some sense the limits or the historical specificity of any form of analysis that might come out of psychoanalysis in its relation towards politics. Now if we agree that certain aspects of desire and identification trouble the world, that there are problems about those identifications, the question we might want to ask is: is it the case historically that it's always the same aspects of desire and identification that trouble the world, or is there some process that's actively changing? So, for example, to put it in another way, when we talk about nationalism people often say say: 'Well, nationalism, in its extreme form is a problem about the relationship of self to other, and through that, a problem about a relationship of self to self.' Now, in that statement we are making essentially a kind of universal claim, which we would have difficulty perhaps, in other contexts, maintaining through historical change. I have in mind the way in which you talk about Freud's struggle with these questions in the shadow of the looming presence of what would be, after he died, the Second World War. The question is: is that kind of struggle that he had then with certain aspects of desire and identification the same one that we have now, when you write about Freud and Abu Ghraib and the Iraq war, for example?

JR. If I could have had a fantasy about the question you would ask me, Henrietta, that would have been it! I don't have a simple answer, but I've become more and more struck by how much Freud is a child of this time. In a way, the whole of his life was shadowed by this rising threat— in 1897 Lueger was confirmed as the anti-Semitic Mayor of Vienna, having been refused by the Emperor three times. It was a historic moment which made clear that the emancipatory tide of the world was being brought to a halt, and the forces of the night were, in a relatively short period of time, going to be marching on the streets. But to say that Freud is a child of a rise in anti-Semitism—and Stephen's written about this better than anybody else in *Hate and the 'Jewish Science'* [2005]—needs immediately to be qualified, in order to stress that it is not anti-Semitism as eternal hostility towards the Jews, but something very specific historically. That concept of eternal hostility towards the Jews is the one that Hannah Arendt considers to be so dangerous. It is the version espoused by Zionism and is being used as we speak to justify violence against the Palestinians. For me, Arendt is our best thinker on this. She warns not to take flight into a myth of eternal anti-Semitism, even when it's hideously confirmed, or appears to be, by history. Instead, she insists that what gave rise to inter-war anti-Semitism was the construction of the stateless person consequent on the First World War, which in turn was tied to a very precise concept of nationalism, German Romantic nationalism, based on an idea of ethnicity, faith, land, blood, descent. For me, the exchange between Freud and Zweig is so graphic because you can see these two men struggling with that concept of nationalism. Freud hates national illusions, because of the

suffering this version of nationalism has caused, is caus-
ing, the Jews. Zweig goes to Palestine in search of a new
national identity, hates what he sees there and leaves. He
makes the decision at a Poale Zion, left-wing demonstra-
tion about the Arab riots, when he turns to somebody in
the crowd and they refuse to reply to him in German. You
had to speak Hebrew because a new nation is being con-
structed with a new language, as if, he adds, they 'didn't
all speak Yiddish at home'. He is fundamentally disen-
chanted by the rigidity of national identity that is forming
around him. So, for me, the fact that Freud is taking
apart identity at the very moment when it is solidifying in
this way, specifically for the Jews, says a lot about how
psychoanalysis' critique of identity is bound up with resur-
gent nationalism.

Now, to get to the second part of your question. Is it
the same in Abu Ghraib? Well, in some ways it's worse,
insofar as what we have in Abu Ghraib is not just the violence of humiliating and exclusive forms of national identity
but also the sadomasochistic pleasure and exhibitionism
that is attached. However, without wishing to equate dis-
parate political moments—US and UK policy on Iraq and
the genesis of Israel as nation—I would want to say that
we can make links. In this case, it is the fiction that allows
us to do so. One of the texts I teach on a course on

Palestine–Israel and fiction is S. Yizhar's incredible short story 'The Prisoner'—I don't know if any of you know it—which was written in 1949, that's to say the year after the Palestinian *nakba* or War of Independence, as Israel terms it. In this story, a group of young Israeli soldiers move in on an idyllic, pastoral, biblical landscape, to seize an Arab shepherd who they are going to send to be tortured. They start humiliating him, and one of the members of the army starts taking pictures of the whole scene. It makes you shudder, because it is like Abu Ghraib. I don't know the answer to the question, but it does seem that there's a kind of rampant self-congratulatory nationalism that tips over into not just blindness towards the other but the necessary dehumanizing and humiliation of the other. If it has its beginnings in German Romantic nationalism, it then migrates to the Middle East—indeed that is one of the tragedies of the conflict.

Something of that structure of national identity and its attendant humiliation, I think Freud is seeing the genesis of, and he predicts it will be catastrophic. He supported the Zionist project of a Hebrew university in Jerusalem, and he talks about the up-building of the land, but he's very wary of what he calls Zionist 'fanaticism' in seizing the Holy Land, famously writing that he wished the Jewish national movement had chosen a 'less historically burdened' land. Something about the emergence of that, and some of its worse psycho-sexual aspects, I feel are still with us, because of course their history is still with us. We are all still the offspring of that moment. The problem of Israel–Palestine has not been resolved. Israel was created ten years after Freud died—he saw its coming and it's still with us. But that doesn't answer what I think is your more radical question about historical change, which presumably refers to going somewhere, focusing on something, other than the West.

HM. Right, but what's troubling me at the moment is that when we are talking about nationalism, we are doing so through an exploration of its most extreme manifestations, the parts of it which we absolutely cannot come to terms with and want to disavow ourselves. And, when we do that, we forget something about it, which is that there are other aspects of nationalism which are about the reservoir of positive values that people have called on in different times and different places to create imaginatively, the communities which have given them sustenance and hope and continuity. In other words—instead of being a theory of death, it becomes a way of life. Now, when you look at the different ways in which that is done at different moments, then you have to look of course at different mechanisms for identification. And, very crucially for a social scientist, you would not only have to look at different mechanisms for identification but also at the very specific contexts in which this identification takes place, and to trace out in each case exactly how they work. In a sense the move which we would make in the social sciences would be very akin to the kind of move that would be made in literature. It's that multiplicity, the idea of the multiple ways in which you can be a national subject, not all of which you understand at every moment and in every context. And I think one wouldn't want to lose that. We have to somehow recuperate positive aspects of building communities and relations with each other.

JR. I agree with you. Quite a few years ago Linda Colley wrote her book *Britons* [1992], in which she talked about the emancipatory and liberal concept of British identity, somewhat against the grain of contemporary thought, let it be said. It must be remembered that Zionism was the movement of national self-determination of the Jewish people. One of the most interesting things about working on Zionism is in fact to discover how multifaceted that impulse could be. Theordor Herzl, who was the founder of political Zionism, most famous for *Der Judenstaat*, wrote a novel called *Altneuland* in 1902, which is a utopia. It was severely criticized for not having enough Jewish content. In fact it's hardly Jewish at all except insofar as it starts in the salons of Vienna with disaffected, upper-middle class Viennese Jewry who would be defined today as self-loathing Jews. He could be accused of anti-Semitism, and he has been of course. He also did not hesitate to take advantage of anti-Semitism to further the claims of Zionism as ridding Europe of its unwanted Jews. But when he gets to Palestine in this fantasy, he creates a community where religious identity is irrelevant to your status as citizen. Well, I wish . . . Students read this and they think: 'Oh my goodness . . . what went wrong?!' It is an idealization, some would argue a wilful self-blinding to what Zionism would necessarily entail, and the view of the (few) Arabs in the book is nothing if not patronizing. But what is intriguing is that, at the same time as Herzl was promoting his version of nationalism as a state for the Jewish people, he seems to allow the space, even if qualified by the European nature of this new colony, for the recognition of the forms of plural identification that you're suggesting.

I think you have to be careful here. For example, I've just been reading Amartya Sen's plea in *Violence and Identity* for forms of identity which would not split along what he calls one 'prioritized line of divisiveness'. And he advocates, celebrates—this time internally to the individual subject—the multiple forms of identity that anyone can have and be. I think there is a problem in that he believes in reason too much. That is to say, he believes in the notion of secular multiple identities based on a concept of reason which then bypasses the unconscious force of identities. So my question back to you is: when you've negotiated all these specific various and changing identities, at what point do they congeal, and one takes precedence? And then, what you do with that?

HM. But I think that they don't freeze all at the same point historically. For a social scientist, what we need to know is why they freeze at a particular time in a particular way and under a particular set of circumstances—and, actually, even getting the data to do that is horrendously difficult. But perhaps, before I let Stephen come back in, we could go back to the relationship between the questions we've been discussing around identification, and the actual context of lives lived, that is, the materiality of circumstances. That's very pressing of course because the electricity has just been turned off in Gaza and all the schools and hospitals are failing. In the social sciences, we'd say we need to put together the injustices of recognition with the injustices of distribution and see how those two things go together, the particular way they reinforce each other under particular kinds of state regimes of power and state institutions. But there's a kind of difficulty there, revealed, I think, in your essay on suicide bombers—which is a very challenging essay and I know that people have talked to you a lot about it—that is, when one tries to understand why people become suicide bombers. Of course, there are a set of explanations about the material circumstances they find themselves in, about the instability of the environment, the emiseration of lives, the lack of recognition. And then there are issues of arguments about the personal histories of the individuals who become suicide bombers and how those personal histories intersect with those larger scenes of political economy. Yet, even when we've done all of that, we still don't know why people become suicide bombers.

JR. I couldn't agree with you more. It reminds me of when I was working on the South African Truth and Reconciliation Commission, and reading the chapter on the perpetrators. First of all, they feel the need to justify including such a chapter; it seems that if you understand someone you're exonerating them, which of course is not true. Then they try to explain. They insist the perpetrators were not motivated by sadism—Gillian Slovo's novel *Red Dust* [2000] is a brilliant reposte since she makes her chief perpetrator a sadist. They insist it is not a question of individual pathology. It's not any of these things, in fact it's to do with group identification. Their terms are

67

compliance, identity, internalization, that is, they give a kind of group psychological reading of why people become perpetrators under apartheid. But just when you have taken in this explanation, they add that it doesn't work, that social identity theory can explain the preconditions of violence, but 'not violence itself'. It's disturbing, to read, because it is as if there's something that disappears through the gaps, in fact, something they cannot reach. So I think what you've just said is terribly important. Derrida would, I think, move in on what you've just described at the speed of light as a theoretical supplement, if you like, something which cannot be grasped in terms of causality at all. Psychoanalysis might refer it to the dark point of the law or what is radically and constitutively unknowable about the mind.

But there is something else, which I only became conscious of as I was writing about suicide bombers. To give the women who carry out these appalling acts a personal history is in a way to insult them—odd as this may sound—as if to say that they were not the agents of their own political history, but manipulated or disappointed women who believed they were going to be united with their fixer in heaven, or were only acting because they'd been betrayed as a woman or were unable to have children and so on. So the more you individualized the women—which one writer saw as a feminist gesture of giving them back their histories—the more you have cut them off from their own sense of political action. There is a crucial distinction between suicide and martyrdom. If you make it personal, then you've turned them into suicides, which is a violation in the Qu'ran. It therefore becomes a very, very vexed question as to which set of explanations you want to use. Finally, I would want to say that there's no final explanation as to why somebody does it. For me, that's a source of comfort—that there's something that can't be finally explained—but not, I suspect, for a social scientist. For me, it stops you falling into the trap of feeling that these acts are something you can too easily control and distance yourself from. In fact, whenever Freud thinks he can explain things that he really knows, he nearly always gets it wrong. To take one of the most famous cases. He really knew that Dora was in love with Herr K, and pushed her to acknowledge that she was, that she had repressed her heterosexual desire for this man, but she wasn't—she was in love with his wife. On the other hand, in all those moments when he admits he doesn't know, then something starts to shimmer on the page and there's more possibilities of the kind you've been talking about earlier.

QUESTION 1. Thank you very much all three of you for the profoundly interesting talks. My question is regarding the psychoanalytic kind of subversion of one's own misery or [projection of] one's own suffering onto other people. Is the same thing happening in Iraq. And, the second strand of my question to all three of you: how could we explain national and international religious sectarian violence, especially with regard to what's happening in Iraq? You know, Pakistanis and Saudis and Sudanese people are deployed in Iraq to kill certain religious factions in the name of some sort of religious nationalism, whereby this specific faction has to govern and rule and that faction cannot have any say whatsoever.

HM. Do you want to have a go at that?

JR. No, I'd like you to.

HM. OK, well, I think this harks back in part to when I was talking about the historical specificity that particular forms of identification have taken and the particular deployment of nationalism in certain kinds of contexts. Because I think that what is happening in Iraq is a very specific kind of deployment of a certain set of identifications, a certain kind of claim about the relation of power to the world. And I don't think that that kind of claim has necessarily taken that form in previous historical moments.

Now, that doesn't mean that there aren't universal aspects to it, the point that Jacqueline was making in reply to me, that is, that fantasy is of necessity a relational thing—it sets up the relation between self and others or between the individual and the collective or between one collective and another collectivity. But I think that what is important is to set those kinds of deployments of anxieties and fears and so on, in the context of specific forms of American imperialism, and the supporters of American imperialism. In exactly the same way I would say that the specific forms of religiosity that we see in the world today have very important connections, of course, to the form in which religiosity has taken in the past perhaps, even to the mediaeval period, but, the particular form that they take, the historical form that they take, is the thing that differentiates them. So we have to in a way find a way of putting this question of how psychoanalysis can be used into specific historical contexts.

JR. I would want to agree with that and I would want to just add two things; one is, just to refer to Karen Armstrong's *The Battle for God* [2000], about the three great fundamentalisms: Protestant, Islamic and Jewish. The point of her book is obviously quite simply that Islam is not the origin of fundamentalism. In fact, as she points out, fundamentalism begins with a set of pamphlets in

America in the 1930s and therefore with a very specific provenance in history. Her argument is also that fundamentalism is the flip-side of secular modernity, which thought it could wipe faith off the face of the earth. I think you have to look very specifically, for example, at the USSR and what has been done to religion in Communist countries. Freud was the worst, by the way in *The Future of an Illusion* [1927]. He thought religion was pure illusion and in the future it would be dispelled by reason. He should have known better since he of all people knows that you don't dispel things just because they're an illusion, in fact you hold onto them all the more.

SF. Only a tiny thing to add, which is about the way in which psychoanalysis can add something to this political dream. Just building slightly on Jacqueline's point then, to think about both the relationship of fundamentalism to secularism—a really key one that gets neglected in popular discourse on fundamentalism—but also about the psychoanalytic notions of investment and identification which have just been drawn on by Jacqueline. Particularly, identification as a mode of placing psychic life into a kind of shell which gives it shape and which stores up the potentially fragile identity as a really important area of looking at how individuals become immersed in fundamentalism.

QUESTION 2. I'm [wondering] if you've seen the denigration of Ken Livingstone. I remember Livingstone supported a priest or imam coming from Saudi Arabia or Egypt, and I think the animosity seems to be extremely intense. What is the motivation? Instead of generating empathy between the different nationalities, different groups . . . this motivation is beyond my understanding.

JR. Well, I think you're saying something very profound about the hounding of Ken Livingstone.[2] He has become the sort of hate valve for his willingness to communicate beyond the barriers of communication that are being policed by the culture. Now, I think what he said, by the way, about the journalist as a concentration camp guard was deeply offensive, so I'm not supporting him on that at all. But I think something about who you can and can't talk to goes to the heart of what we've been discussing this evening. Because it's as if the very process of a verbal exchange involves either an identification or a contamination and the popular culture is trying to police the boundaries very rigidly of what is communicable and what should and shouldn't be understood. I think that's what you're talking about and I think we need to be very wary of it indeed.

HM. But I also think there's another part of it, and its something which Freud alluded to when he talked about the narcissism of minor differences. When the Greeks and Turks in Cyprus were asked why they were fighting each other, they replied, 'Well, because we smoke different kinds of cigarettes.' There is a sense in which the need to create that difference between communities has now become urgent. As if those differences have to be forced all the time. I think now we are in a situation where people are seeking to drive those divisions and they drive them more the more they feel connected to each other—and that's the paradox. I think that's particularly the case with the relationship between the Christian and the Muslim faiths, many of whose precepts are actually remarkably close to each other.

JR. And of course that link—historical and potential—was part of what Edward Said was drawing on at the end of his life when he and Daniel Barenboim formed the West-Eastern Divan Orchestra—he said it was his most important work—which is to get musicians in a room together from Israel and the surrounding Arab countries and they play music, and then they also have discussions. They have to talk about it, I mean it's not just 'let's make music together', although that is a great deal, but it's a very complex endeavour.

QUESTION 3. One of the key sentences in *The Question of Zion* is when you write: 'Let's do what psychoanalysis does, to escape this "you are either with it or against it" and accept that it's [Zionism] a symptom'—I think that's an interesting approach to open up a new space to work through the many shades there are, and look at what it is. Coming back to the relationship between psychoanalysis and politics: I was just wondering to what extent you understand it? Not as putting a nation on the couch, but almost as an epistemological or methodological device, insofar as it breaks up the policing of boundaries and spaces that cannot be talked about.

JR. I think you are asking if I use psychoanalysis as a kind of epistemological device for opening up what I think is the interval of reflection in the sense that Stephen described it. Much more specifically, just to fill in, that questioner was referring to a moment in a book I wrote on Zionism, *The Question of Zion*, where I cite the poet and critic Tom Paulin who said: 'Look, you're either a Zionist or an anti-Zionist, there's no middle way.'[3] In response to what felt to me like a false choice, I summarize the thought of Russian formalist, Viktor Shklovsky: 'There is no third path, and that is the one we're going to take'; he was referring to the aesthetic options officially available in the Soviet Union in the 1930s and I found his remark very suggestive. I was trying to open up to a space where you can be critical of Zionism at the same time as entering into an understanding of the basic project. It requires a political version of 'suspension of disbelief'. We're so often presented with false alternatives, so for example, you're not meant to talk about the suffering of the Jewish people and their injustice or violent treatment of the Palestinians in the same breath—you're meant to either acknowledge one, or acknowledge the other. I'm interested in a world in which you can get these incompatibles on the same page and then see what happens to the way people think about their identities and what they're doing with them.

This, I do think, has real political, not just epistemological, resonances. In last week's *Haaretz*, Doron Rosenblum, who is one of my favourite columnists, took a statement by Foreign Minister Tzipi Livni when Bush was in Israel last week. It was a text she had written and given to Bush in response to his remark: 'I will never be able to feel what it is to be a Jew or an Israeli. I can only imagine but I will never be able to truly know what it is like.' Livni wrote: 'To be a Jew is to dream the Holocaust, to live the Holocaust, to die the Holocaust—without having been there.' He just took it apart syntactically as a way of asking what it means to say: 'This is what it is to be Jewish'; that this reality in some way exhausts the identity of Israeli and Jew. What has happened to identity when you do that and what, we might add, is then licensed by way

of dehumanizing—cutting off electricity to the
Palestinians—as a consequence. Rosenblum asked: 'Was
the goal to obtain more airplanes?' Had the founding of
the state not changed a thing in the definition of 'the
Hebrew man', only deepened his notion of victimhood,
by exchanging the nations of Europe for the Arabs: 'Is the
arming of the Jewish community in Israel the sum total of
the meaning of the State of Israel?' So for me these questions of how you see yourself psychically, and what then
you do politically, are absolutely inseparable. I think you
put it beautifully but I hope it can go a bit further than
that. I like to think it has further effects.

QUESTION 4. I've been sort of a pained observer of the
Palestinian situation since the late Seventies really and in
every way their situation has got worse I think, the land is
less, their dignity is destroyed. Edward Said said a long
time ago that Palestine is a country of words, and that still
remains the case, doesn't it? That there isn't a Palestine
and it remains a country of words. And I think one of the
things which is very difficult for me to contain over the
years is a sense of anger and outrage. There's been a kind
of a semiotic conquest as well as a military conquest of
Palestine, and that's very difficult to resist, isn't it, when
very powerful nations collude with the oppression of
another nation?

JR. I partly agree with you, but do not see it as a complete semiotic victory. Yitzhak Laor, who I think is one of the strongest Israeli commentators on the scene, has said that everyone in Israel cannot help but imbibe the language of the state, that is the available, dominant, narrative. To that extent he would agree with you, that there is a kind of semiotic victory. But on the Palestine–Israel course that I'm involved in, we read Emile Habiby, Mahmoud Darwish, Anton Shamas, Sayed Kashua and so on—the writing coming out of Palestine is extraordinary and incredibly radical and subversive. As are the films, such as Elia Suleiman's *Divine Intervention* [2002], Hany Abu-Assad's *Paradise Now* [2005], Juliano Mer Khamis' *Arna's Children* [2003], Asher Tlalim's *Galoot* [2003] and many more. So I don't want to be too negative, even though I agree with the situation being politically a catastrophe. I would also want to refer to Karma Nabulsi's incredible project over the last few years, collating the voices of all the Palestinians in the Diaspora in the Civitas Project.[4] Said always used to say that it's not just the words—there is also the affirmation of an identity, or peoplehood as Palestinian, in the teeth of the most incredible attempts to erase it completely. We can take a little bit of hope, I think, from that persistence, that resistance we might say, to go back to the beginning. So I agree with you up to a point but I don't want to be quite as depressed.

QUESTION 5 [SHAHIDHA BARI]. I want to try and encourage you to put back together your fractured and broken subject as alluring as it is. Is there something to recommend the put-together subject, or the strong subject?—Insofar as the one thing I wish someone had said to Mohammed Atta or Mohammed Sadiq Khan or to many of the children in his classroom would be to believe in the possibility of effecting change in the world by living in it rather than dying in it. And there are perhaps certain beliefs and principles that are unimpeachable and that shouldn't be broken. And I wonder whether the broken and fractured subject, as beautiful as it is, might also need some strong impregnable beliefs, a kind of a will, and whether we need to cultivate that too?

JR. Well it's a brilliant question and you've asked me it before—Shahidha's been part of the Graduate Forum I organize with Daniel Pick that I mentioned before. When we've been talking, say, about Judith Butler's appeal for the melancholic subject, you've said, if you don't mind me quoting you back at yourself, that this notion of the melancholic subject is a problem if we're talking about political self-affirmation in the face of injustice. This was an argument that went on in feminism throughout the Seventies and Eighties when first there was the demand for an assertive ego on the part of women and then the

critique of precisely those forms of assertion. Virginia
Woolf argued in *Three Guineas* that if you join the men's
procession, you will go to war, which is to say that the last
thing that we want is for women to have egos like men. So
there's a real problem here. When there is an emiserated,
deprived, unequal subject, what does it mean to say of the
subject: be fragmented when actually what they need is to
be strong, coherent subjects and affirm themselves? In
the case of feminism, the demand can even seem complicit with the disabling stereotype of women as never
holding things, or indeed themselves, together. On that I
agree with you. But I would want to say there's affirmation and affirmation. Somebody humiliated, who feels
that their community is being abjected by the dominant
culture, needs to affirm themselves—this is what I think
Said was talking about, the demand for justice and recognition—but without that identity seizing up, which is
another form of death. Your question is *the* question. How
do you prise apart, as well as maintain, both? So this is a
perfect moment in a way for us to draw to a conclusion as
it relates back to Henrietta's question as to what could be
a form of national identity that would be positive in its
sense of the enablement of a subject in history, without
becoming politically frozen or petrified, without, I would
want to add, licensing violence against another people in

the name of its own historic, even if necessary, empowerment. It is a question central to Jewish history, because
the Jews were a persecuted people, who wanted, needed,
national self-determination. What went wrong? So the
book ends with a tribute to my sister's thought, Gillian
Rose, who asked, in relation to Jewishness: 'What could
be an ethical form of holding on to power?' That was the
question Israel began with, and it has failed its own question, drastically.

QUESTION 6. The Jews being a people as we know, and
being Jewish, as well as a great possible self-knowledge
and reflection, and so on, and what we know about psychoanalysis and the Jews—why [has it] gone so badly
wrong and what, this is the second part, do you suggest
could be done to try and raise the consciousness of the
Israeli people to what's been going on? I know very well
that the Israelis are totally blind to the plight of the
Palestinians—well, many, many of them. They are blink-
ered and they don't want to know the Palestinians, [or]
what they're going through. And they talk about 'the
Arabs' and that's it, and I wondered if you have any positive ideas that you might tell us about now?

JR. International pressure—I know that sounds like a very,
very naive answer to your very complex question. Unless

there's international pressure on Israel, nothing's going to change; unless their way of seeing themselves trans- forms itself, nothing is going to change, and that's why I think it is an ideological as well as a political question. When you enter into this field, you get hostility of the kind you get in no other field—people lie about you, they really lie about what you're saying. Avi Shlaim has been the target of a lot of criticism and hostility for writing *The Iron Wall*. When I put the question to him, he said it's because it really is a political issue. If you criticize Israel, you are seen by Israel as damaging its image in the world which will then undermine its standing and what it can do. That's why—to plug Independent Jewish Voices— which I'm proud to be part of—we like to think that what we're saying is quite important: that it's OK to be Jewish and be critical, not just those of us who have access to the media but far more widely. It may damage the image of Israel for now, but not at the cost of a long-term future for Israel, certainly not at the cost of the continuing possi- bilities of an ethical way of being Jewish. To go back to your point about Palestine being a nation of writers—it is a struggle over words, but you know, I wouldn't be a literary person if I didn't think the struggle over words mattered.

HM. Well, we've come to just after eight o'clock which is actually the end of our allotted time. I think that

Jacqueline has nicely brought us back to the point where we began, so perhaps we will stop there. I would just like to thank both Stephen Frosh and Jacqueline Rose for coming to the LSE tonight and talking to us about these very important matters, and I would like to urge you to go and buy a copy of Jacqueline's book and come to the next event of Psychoanalysis@LSE. Thank you all very much.

JR. Thank you, Henrietta, and Stephen too.

HENRIETTA MOORE is the William Wyse Professor of Social Anthropology, University of Cambridge, and Director of the Culture and Globalization Programme of the Centre for the Study of Global Governance at the London School of Economics. STEPHEN FROSH is Pro-Vice Chancellor and Head of the School of Psychosocial Studies at Birkbeck University of London.

Notes

1   Henrietta Moore, *The Subject of Anthropology: Gender, Symbolism and Psychoanalysis* (Cambridge: Polity Press, 2007), p. 17.

2   Former Mayor of London, renowned for his outspoken opinions, who invited Yusuf al-Qaradawi to speak in London. Qaradawi had defended Palestinian suicide

bombers while condemning the 7 July bombings in London. He is also known for his homophobic views.

3   In 'The Sound and the Fury', an interview by Sean O'Hagan, *The Observer*, 20 January 2002. Available at: www.guardian.co.uk/books/2002/jan/20/poetry.features

4   *Palestinians Register: Laying Foundations and Setting Directions* (Report of the Civitas Project) (Oxford: Nuffield College, 2006).

THE BOUNDS AND LIMITS OF IDENTITY

A CONVERSATION WITH SUPRIYA CHAUDHURI AND AVEEK SEN
KALA KUNJ, CALCUTTA, 6 JANUARY 2008

SUPRIYA CHAUDHURI (SC). Good evening, everyone. It's a
great pleasure to be here, and I am honoured to have
been invited to this occasion. By way of introduction to
Jacqueline and her works, I'll begin by asking you,
Jacqueline, something about the form that you character-
istically choose for your writing. I've always very much
been struck by the form of the essay, which you seem to
have made your own, sometimes without footnoting,
which is even more accessible and a real pleasure to read,
and sometimes with the academic adjunct of footnotes—
but always allowing a thread to be carried through to an
end, which remains somewhat speculative, somewhat
open, but provides the satisfaction of the short piece.

87

JACQUELINE ROSE (JR). Some of the answer to this is contingent. I have been very privileged for the last ten years or so to be a contributor to the *London Review of Books*, whose format is deliberately non-academic and without footnotes. But I am sure it goes back to much earlier, when the inspirational frames for thinking were the radical journals of the Seventies in London, such as *New Left Review*, *Screen* magazine, and then later *m/f*, the feminist theoretical journal. *Screen* was absolutely decisive, because it was a film theory magazine into which French theory and critical thought entered long before they entered into English literary studies, where there was the cultural tradition of F. R. Leavis, with his stress on the moral and elite dimension of literature, and a certain weight of tradition. Whereas film culture had barely got into universities and, therefore, could be much more experimental. My first affiliations were with those radical journals, none of which, crucially, were university presses, and the essay was the automatic format for that context. I think that marked me for life. Today, the essay form is often the result of a spoken occasion. I like the idea of taking people on a journey, and your description of the essays as open-ended. Juliet Mitchell once said to me that she only ever writes when she feel there's something that she doesn't understand. That's what makes her start writing. It influenced me profoundly.

AVEEK SEN (AS). There is also about the essay a certain presentness, even if you're discussing the past, even if you're being historical, which opens out into the topical, the contemporary. Is that how you see the essay form as well?

JR. The question of the tense in which you write is fascinating, and leads to the question of psychoanalysis which I know we will be coming to later. I have always been very struck by Lacan's definition of the time of analysis as the future perfect, which is in a way an impossible tense: what I will have been. He's arguing against the idea that psychoanalysis is about the past, in some simple, completed sense. The time of analysis is not the past of what I once was and am no more, which would be repression, nor the past of what I was and still am, which would be repetition. It's what I will have been for what I am in the process of becoming. You're looking back and trying to move forward at the same time, as you discover the past through the present by means of which you engage it—a strange notion of time which I've never thought about before in relationship to the essay form. This goes back of course, to Freud's very early paper, 'Screen Memories' [1899], where he says nobody has a memory of their childhood because we endlessly call up our memories at the point of time when we need them. There is no such thing as simply a memory. I think the essay form allows you to call up that part of the past that is needed now.

sc. Yes. If I may, I felt that very strongly in the essay you wrote in the memory of your sister Gillian Rose,[1] because there is this sense at its end of anxiously consulting someone who is in the past and still has something to say, or might provide advice or counsel. That feeling is so strong at the end of that essay . . . very moving. And many of your essays have that quality. Of ending on a particularly personal, engaged moment, which is still not a conclusion.

JR. The particular occasion of that essay was the tenth anniversary of her death being observed in a very public space—the Institute of Contemporary Arts in London— with a motley crew, to say the least: the Archbishop of Canterbury; Howard Caygill, the philosopher; the novelist Maggie Gee; and the social theorist, David Held in the Chair. We were all accumulating visions of Gillian Rose in complex and interrelated ways.

I think one of the things that Gillian was arguing was that the split between civil society and the state was utterly debilitating for contemporary political life. She didn't like those modern theorizations which, in response to the current corruption of what Hannah Arendt called the 'reason of state', take flight in some way, either into writing, or some poeticized conception of Judaism, or into the Unconscious. She wanted to bring back the question of power from which, she believed, you could not absent yourself. The question that then has to be asked, in relation to my own interest in Israel–Palestine, is: what could be a form of empowerment that does not corrupt and brutalize itself? It seems to me to be the urgent contemporary political question for Israel at the moment. So the ending of that essay has a particular urgency, almost like 'Please tell me what you think.' As basic as that. And I'm still waiting for her to tell me.

SC. Elsewhere in *The Last Resistance* (which, along with *Sexuality in the Field of Vision* [1986], has come out in an Indian edition),[2] you quote Said, who says: 'There is suffering and injustice enough for everyone.'[3] That is so important in understanding any history of partition and the creation, the birth, of a new state. While it may be that some of the writers that you refer to are not well known to Indian readers, nevertheless the issues that you engage with are so well known, so familiar to us from our own histories and memories, that I felt at every point in that book that there is something I can bring to this by way of personal feeling and analogy.

JR. Well, as I was preparing to come here, I was reading Amartya Sen and Shashi Tharoor. There are incredible moments of analogy which I hadn't been fully aware of before. In *India: From Midnight to the Millennium and Beyond* [1997], Tharoor quotes one of the intellectual godfathers of Hindutva, 'Veer' Savarkar, as saying that the Hindu is a person who sees the land between the Indus and the sea as his fatherland as well as his Holy Land, and he analyses that passage as the sacralization of the land and of the nation. That could have been lifted out of a piece of Zionist writing. The problem is not the love of the land, but the land becoming a sacred object to which one set of people then have divine entitlement. More and more I can see these profound analogies around the question of partition and of the land.

In relation to Said's statement—'There is suffering and injustice enough for everyone'—it is such a simple statement, isn't it? and yet so profound. Because the more I study the Israel–Palestine question, the more I realize that central to it are competing narratives of pain. Obviously, for the Israeli people the Jews are permanent sufferers throughout history, and therefore also permanently endangered. But that claim to the monopoly of suffering and to the uniqueness of suffering leads to a blindness towards the suffering of the Palestinian people, as well as to a vision of Jewish history as a continuity of pain. It's like a mental set that is locked, and which creates devastating consequences. Arendt brilliantly wrote about this when she warned in the Thirties and Forties that we must not see anti-Semitism as eternal, because to do so is to detach yourself from politics and history. Anti-Semitism then becomes a mythical status of who I am, which means you cannot see anybody else. Said made the statement in 1997, in an article published in four Arab newspapers—and it was the only time in his life when he received hate mail in the Arab press, because he'd said that it is one of the tasks of the Palestinians to understand the suffering of the Jewish people. It was therefore a very brave statement.

On that question if I may just add this: there is an expression that I would really like to see an end to, and that is the phrase 'Jewish suffering'. I'm happy with the expression 'the Jewish history of suffering' or 'the history of the suffering of the Jewish people', but the phrase 'Jewish suffering' makes me tremble, because it implies that there is a quality of suffering that is uniquely Jewish. There is no doubt that Jews have often been victims of history but, for me, victimhood is an event. It is something that happens to you. The moment it becomes an identity, psychological or political, then I think you're finished.

This is as important for me in relation to feminism as it is in relation to Zionism. We need to be endlessly vigilant in not allowing victimhood to become who I am, completely. Because I think the latter is a disaster.

AS. I think in your writing there is a very natural shift from the notion of identity to identification, especially passionate identification. And identification is both a thrilling activity but also a highly risky one, which is why we are always extending the borders of identification but also setting limits to it. Would you like to comment on that? And also, who sets the limits?

JR. Who sets the limits? Two things come to mind. One is Diana Fuss's book *Identification Papers* [1995], in which she makes a distinction between identity—bad—and identification—good—to crudely simplify a very complex argument. Basically she says that identity is something that fossilizes. I think of it as a symptom in the Freudian sense. The reason for getting rid of the symptom is that it is so expensive psychically: the amount of energy spent propping up the symptom leaves you with no time to go anywhere else in your mind. That is how I think of identity, with one crucial qualification—that we cannot live without it. When Lacan says at the beginning of one of his seminars: 'I wish to create subjects such that the ego does not exist,' he knows he can't do that. Identities can also be facilitating and enabling, although that is not his point. In *Violence and Identity* [2006], Amartya Sen repeats something he's been saying for many years—that it is OK to have an identity but to please have more than one.

AS. Have a whole wardrobe . . .

JR. Beautiful! Thank you! Let's have wardrobes of identities. And let it not matter if they clash, or don't all fit together in some straightforward way, although even here we have to be wary, be careful not to idealize a plurality of identities as if they settle the more difficult issue: that it is the definition of an identity that it monopolizes the psychic space and rigidifies. Identification, on the other hand, is something quite else. With identification, you give up a part of yourself because you go over to the other side. One of Mikkel Borch-Jakobsen's best articles is 'The Freudian Subject, from Politics to Ethics'.[4] I don't know if he is known here, he was a brilliant Freudian commentator who then turned against Freud and went over to hypnosis. In that early paper, he talks about narcissism in Freud, and the proposition that can be lifted from the idea of narcissism that 'I am the same as the Other,' making the point that there are two ways of conjugating that sentence. One is that the Other basically has to be the same as me, which he calls politics, and then fascism, which to him had become the same thing. The other one is that I am the same as the Other: I destitute myself by going over to the other side, which he calls ethics as it is, in some profound sense, the recognition of your own death. And it's true that if you really identify with the Other—some people would argue that you can never do it, but try, just try—I think the concrete political effects can be profound. During the First Gulf War, during the final 'turkey shoot', which, as we all know, since the war was already won, was unnecessary—there was absolutely no reason to strafe the ground in the way that the Americans did at the end of that war—a group of American helicopter pilots were asked: 'How do you feel to be killing all those people?' One of them replied something along the lines: 'First of all, I don't think about it. And secondly, I am glad that I am on the right side and part of a Godly nation.' You could just see the fossilizing of a self-righteous identity which allowed him to kill blindly. Perhaps naively, I think that if you allow yourself to identify with the Other or enemy, you cannot kill, because then it would be a piece of yourself that you're killing.

Death is therefore present twice. You die a little to identify, but then it means you can't, or can less easily, cause the other to die. There is a moment in one of

Seagull's recent books *Violence and Democracy in India* which comes close to this, where Martha Nussbaum is talking about the particular violence against women that took place during the Gujarat mass violence against Muslims in 2002, and she suggests that in destroying the Other, you are destroying the possibility of your own death.[5] Something has to be utterly evicted. The contemporary psychoanalyst Christopher Bollas makes a similar point in his essay on the structure of evil in *Cracking Up*,[6] that the killer is trying to transcend his own death. So, to go back to your question Aveek, which I have been meandering around . . .

AS. Please meander more . . .

JR. I think identification as a type of crossing over is a challenge, but also one of the hardest things to do because we have character-armour. In one of Amartya Sen's pieces, he quotes Isaiah Berlin citing Rabindranath Tagore, who on the one hand expressed his belief in a kind of cosmopolitanism, suggesting that Indians should give up on rigid, traditional identities, which he compares to being tethered to the past like a goat—that they should be open even to American influence—but on the other insisted that if there is any risk of becoming American and denying your Indianness then it would be better to stay in a locked room.[7] It is that complex mediation between two positions that exclude each other by definition which is the balance that is so hard to get right, although balance is not the right word. I don't think any of us manages it in any simple way.

SC. But I think Tagore did to some extent at least, and it reminds me that at critical moments, these writers and thinkers seem to have come together and had something to say which could bear upon other people's views. For example, I remember Gandhi speaking about the rights of the Palestinian Arabs. In 1938, he comments that although the Palestinians should have adopted non-violent means, their position is absolutely justified. And then there is Tagore's very very strong opposition to nationalism, the modern nation-state, which he calls an apparatus of terrifying power and cannibalistic zeal. There is an extraordinary set of statements that you can take out of Tagore recording his bitter hostility to the nation-state. You can see these writers as anticipating what history now is making so plain.

JR. One of the fascinating things for me about working on Zionism was reading not just Hannah Arendt but also Martin Buber and Ahad Ha'am. He is very little known outside Israel, but is taught in schools there. First of all, it's chilling: their predictions of what is going to happen, especially Arendt's, exactly as you say with Tagore. It reads like a description of today: for example, that the nation will come to rely entirely on a foreign power, probably America, which wasn't true at that time at all because, up until Israel's victory in the 1967 war, America was in fact highly ambivalent about Israel. The prescience of it is stunning. But more precisely, it is the way these writers sense—exactly as Tagore—that the nation-state is a very dangerous apparatus. In the midst of the Zionist moment, Buber asks: 'Where does truth and justice determine our deeds?' He also says: in our individual lives we are fully human, but we are leading political lives that are less than human. He is appealing to Jewish tradition throughout, to counter a certain notion of statehood and empowerment. Now, of course, a certain Zionist Right would say: 'Here you go again—you are saying that you should be passive, that you should be without power—look where that got us.' You can see how complex this argument is. But, crucially, for the critics what was involved was also a critique of nationalism, and a fear that if nationalism fossilizes into a singular identity, then the nation, in Hans Kohn's words, will 'take out the bayonets'. To get back to Aveek's question—it would have to defend those constricted bounds of national identity that it has belligerently fossilized into place.

AS. Talking about states, in your book *States of Fantasy* [1996] there are two states: one is Palestine, and the other is South Africa. Could you tell us a bit about that journey that you make?

JR. The South Africa story is again personal and partly contingent. When I was at Sussex University, I saw my task as introducing feminism into the inter-disciplinary courses that were being taught. We started up a course called 'Studies in Feminism' that included women's social history—the story, for example, of women's labour in the mines in nineteenth-century England, socio-biology, eugenics, and then psychoanalysis. I was so focused on this project as a political task, which met with a lot of resistance in the beginning—it was seen, rightly I should say, as biased, as in 'pro-feminist' (for that reason we had deliberately called it 'Studies *in* Feminism' not 'Studies *on* Feminism' to make it clear that feminism was the subject, not just the object, of the course)—that for several years I completely ignored the struggle over getting women writers onto the mainstream English Literature curriculum. It was not where I put my energy. Someone pointed out it was a little inconsistent, to say the least. I didn't need much persuading. So we set up a women's writing course. However, if I did not focus on this first, I think it is also because I'd always had trouble with the concept of

'women's writing' as an entity on its own, because if feminism is right, that women are subordinated to patriarchal
values, then there is no woman writer who will not be in
dialogue with a male writer in some sense, and I prefer
the idea of watching how that dialogue and interaction
works. However, I was persuaded. Then somebody else
pointed out to me—we're talking about the Seventies
here—that Zora Neale Hurston and Maya Angelou were
missing, to which somebody added: 'And, by the way, you
should read Bessie Head.' I'd never heard of Bessie
Head. So, I read this amazing Botswanan writer—South
African, but she goes into exile in Botswana—whose most
famous book, *A Question of Power* [1974] makes Sylvia
Plath read like a Sunday School tea party. It was so graphic,
so political. Head was not strictly a Cape Coloured
because that term refers to the offspring of the Dutch and
the indigenous Blacks of the seventeenth and eighteenth
centuries, but she came from the Cape and she was
coloured. The rumour is—although it has been contested
—that she was the child of her White mother and the
Black groom, and that this was such a scandal that her
mother was ostracized from the family, sent into a mental
home. Several times Bessie Head was sent out to a foster
home, then sent back because the foster parents thought
they were getting a mixed-race child and she was too
black. So, she is a coloured woman who cannot bear the

Black or the White side of her identity, and who disintegrates under the pressure. It was from there that my interest in South African literature and history began. I started basically to educate myself.

But the focus on South Africa also arose from a feeling, which I still have, that the introduction of Black writing/New Literatures into the English curriculum was predominantly from here, Asia and America. I felt that Britain had at least as much to answer for in relationship to South Africa, and subsequently Israel and Palestine, that the histories being introduced by the introduction of these other literatures were therefore partial, and that there were other places—South Africa and the Middle East—that needed as much attention.

sc. May I ask you to comment just for a minute on the 'Truth and Reconciliation Commission' and the notion of *ubuntu*. What exactly is connoted by this term, which is constantly used and glossed in various ways, none of which appear to be entirely adequate? It is obviously extremely important and I find myself struggling with it, not unhappy with the fact that I don't quite know what it means but I would like to know what your views are.

jr. I think if we could answer this here, then we would probably have destroyed the concept. So let's start by acknowledging this is a moment of real cultural difference that we have to struggle with. The Truth and Reconciliation Commission was a unique experiment, a kind of psychoanalytic cathartic exercise in public. There have been Truth Commissions all across the world, but this was the first one that held its hearings in public. That was the fascination for me. The idea that discourse in a public place could in some sense not cleanse but nonetheless bring to the surface forms of violence, criminality and destitution that the temptation would be otherwise to suppress and wipe out of the historical record. The Commission called that side of their work reducing the number of lies. In the sense of putting on record what happened, it was a huge success. In the sense of reparation, I think it was probably not. But that is to be simple about something much more complex.

Desmond Tutu was the key person in this—he chaired the Commission—and of course, he is Christian. In the Appendix to the Commission Report, dissenting Commissioner Wynand Malan criticizes the Commission for its Christian concept of forgiveness. *Ubuntu* or *Ubuntu botho* is the other side of that—something he does not allude to—so it is in fact wrong to criticize the Commission for being purely Christian, nor do I think it was promoting some blanket or simple notion of forgiveness. As far as I understand it—and this relates back crucially to Aveek's point about identification—*Ubuntu* is to do with the fact that you are nothing or nobody except through people. Now, there's a sloppy sentimental reading of that, which is 'People need people.' In fact, there's a song 'People who need people are the luckiest people in the world.' I am not going to sing it! *Ubuntu* is not about people needing people, because that means the person already exists and then is in need of others. Whereas what is implied by *Ubuntu* is that you are not who you are—in fact you are not at all, except through the Other. It contains no Western notion of a pre-constituted individual subjectivity to whom things then happen and which then reaches out for connection, which is, after all, slightly arrogant: 'Here I am, and I need you.' *Ubuntu* is therefore a very profound critique of Western individualism. Mark Sandler has written about it, through Derrida. There is also a link here to the Borch-Jakobsen article we were discussing earlier which argues that ethics arises when you destitute yourself in the place of the Other. As I understand them, these moments are all trying to gesture towards the idea of being a person without being one, that is to say, without a defensive, narcissistic, selfsame identity. 'Is there a way of being someone without propriety?' would be another version of the same question. So we have everything to learn from *Ubuntu*, even if we don't completely understand it.

More simply I think it has to do with a very different notion of community. In *Country of My Skull* [1998]—the amazing book on the Commission by Antjie Krog, I don't know if it's come out here—she has a chapter on the moment in the Truth Commission when Winnie Mandela was on the witness stand. Of course, the consensus is that Winnie Mandela lied and that she was involved in some appalling practices. But one of the commentators in Krog's book says that you have to understand the difference between a culture of guilt and a culture of shame. A culture of guilt says you must speak the truth and atone for your sins. A culture of shame says you do not speak if it degrades your community. And therefore what a Western vision will see as a lie can be read as a piece of dignified behaviour on the part of the community you represent, which is not to deny what she did. I feel very shaky about these things, which I think are to be learnt and relearnt all the time.

sc. Identity is always fictional, isn't it? So, the problem about understanding identities is that because they are always projections, you should never assume that anyone's speaking the truth. I mean that's the point, isn't it?

jr. Well, Lacan says famously that the species specificity— to use a horrible expression—of the human being is that they can lie. A great deal of effort was put into establish-

105

ing that bees have a language, because they arrive back at the hive and put their bodies in a certain direction to signal where the honey is. Except that, as linguists have pointed out, this is not language in the human sense because the sign is indexical rather than arbitrary—the body is showing which way to go—and the response to the sign is an action and not another sign. So bee language does not compare with human language. Likewise, although there are species that masquerade and deceive, they do not lie. So, for Lacan, what specifies human language is that we can lie. The best illustration of this for me is the example Freud uses in *Jokes and Their Relation to the Unconscious* [1905] (like many of the jokes in the book, the joke can be read as anti-Semitic, although we have to remember that Freud is a Jew): two Jews meet on a train. One says to the other: 'Where are you going?', and the other one says: 'I'm going to Crakow', to which the first replies along the lines: 'Why are you telling me you're going to Crakow, so that I think you're going to Lemberg, when in fact you are going to Crakow? So why are you lying to me?' In the standard edition, this is indexed 'Truth, a Lie (Jewish)'. If you think psychoanalytically, this touches on a radical truth about ourselves. The really radical, disorientating, Freudian question is not, '*What* speaks in the Unconscious?'—in the sense of what has been buried which I might retrieve and speak—but, '*Who speaks in the Unconscious?*' There is more than one person in your mental home. I like to think that if you acknowledge that about the precariousness of your own identity, then you will be closer to a form of identity that can identify. Because if you're Other to yourself, then others are not so Other—a point Julia Kristeva has made.

AS. With this notion of deceiving oneself, I want to bring you back to the key word in this book—'resistance'. There are, in a sense, broadly two meanings to it. One is 'politically opposing something'. The other is 'to thwart oneself, to not confront something, to resist knowing something'. How do you think the two 'inmix'—to use your word in the Sylvia Plath book [*The Haunting of Sylvia Plath*, 1991]—in this book?

JR. That's a very difficult question, because I wanted to use the concept of resistance, above all, to indicate the way the mind thwarts everything that we've been trying to talk about so far this evening. I think it's very important not to idealize psychoanalysis as a radical discourse, not just because Freud was conservative about certain issues, which of course he was, although I do think he was one of the greatest revolutionary thinkers of our time. There is another reason, linked to the idea which a lot of us—

feminists and others interested in the subversive potential of Freud—had in the Seventies and Eighties, the some- what simplified belief that there is the ego, and there is the Unconscious, and that the Unconscious is this site of all the radical alternative forms of identity, specifically sexual identities. Therefore what we want is to dissolve the ego in favour of these forms of sexual freedom. To put it very simply, everybody knows whether they are a man or a woman—everyone knows which door, 'Ladies' or 'Gents', to go through—but the Unconscious knows better. That is for me a formula, one I often use, that sums up what Freud is saying about sexuality. So there was a kind of immense excitement about the radical potential of that insight, but I feel we left something out, and that was the superego. There's not just the ego and the Unconscious, there's the superego through which we take on the identifications that are bestowed upon us, and through which we police our inner world. And, at that point, everything becomes much, much harder. Because the superego instructs people to marshal their identities, to create, if you like, a nation-state formation of our own minds. That's where identity fossilizes and freezes and also becomes violent. Because the superego—and this is, for me, another strand of Freud's genius on sexual mat- ters—is abrasive and sadistic in the mind. There is what

Slavoj Žižek, after Lacan, would call 'the obscenity of the law'. We are required to identify as social subjects with something that is coercive and inherently damaging.

So the first point of *The Last Resistance* was to set a limit, as Freud himself did, to his original thinking, early on in *Studies on Hysteria* [1895]. That, for example, you would just retrieve a memory and the symptom would go; or, as some have deduced from his thought, if you acknowledge your inherent bisexuality, things will be a lot easier for you. Freud was never euphoric. He always said that the most that he could do was turn hysterical misery into common everyday unhappiness. That was about as ambitious as he got. Nonetheless, in that earlier political moment of which I formed a part, there was a kind of belief in an almost magical transformation of the self. I felt I wanted to track the way as he went through his life, faced with not one but two world wars—he died three weeks after the outbreak of the Second World War—that optimism was no longer justified. He was up against what he theorized as Thanatos, or the death drive, and the ability of Thanatos, or the violent side of who we are, to grind identities into shape. What he saw happening at the end of his life was a most dreadful corrective to any utopian belief in psychoanalytic transformation. So, the point of *The Last Resistance* is to say: 'Please slow down and please acknowledge the intractability of the difficulty of the human mind, because if you don't, you're going to have a naive belief in transformation, which then won't happen.'

In this context, I was very interested in the book *The Phobic and the Erotic*, another recent Seagull Books publication,[8] in which I noticed at moments a kind of utopianism about alternative sexualities. I have only understood today that one of the reasons for this is that homosexuality has been so identified with HIV and negativized in India that it is very important to present it in positive, almost jubilatory, terms, if you like. I understand the political need for that move but, for me, there is then a risk of ignoring the complexity and the psychic difficulty of any sexual identity. It is as if, at moments, the psychic is being taken out of the sexual. An example: I know there was a huge controversy about the film *Fire* [1996] here in India about ten years ago. My understanding is that—correct me if I'm wrong—the two women who have a lesbian relationship are both in very unhappy marriages and then they find each other, and that one of the criticisms of the film is that it makes lesbianism contingent on a couple of ghastly blows in life, instead of which lesbianism should have been a self-affirming free thing that will find itself and transform the world in some way. So the film was being reproached for not being positive enough, for not offering a strong enough model of sexual identity. For me, sexual identity is always fraught. There is always psychic pain. As Judith Butler of course has written about at length, as a corrective or sequel, as she would say, to the voluntarism of *Gender Trouble* [1990], there's always an abjection, a melancholic refusal of the aspects of identity you decline or push aside. It is a violent process that leaves its traces, of necessity, in the mind. What I would want to stress more, at the same time, is that sexualities and fantasies are always available for coercion by historic forces in more or less ugly ways. So, resistance is there as a reminder, if you like: a reminder that our psychic identities are not as mobile as we would like them to be. I think we left that out in the earlier turn to Freud.

Having said that, there is resistance in the other sense, which is political resistance. When I gave that paper at the LSE for a conference called 'Flesh and Blood: Psychoanalysis, Politics and Resistance', I sent in my title 'The Last Resistance' and the organizer produced a poster depicting a Palestinian climbing over the wall! And I said: 'No, that's not what I mean: I just want a picture of the wall.' And he said: 'No. Your title is "The Last Resistance", so we must have a Palestinian breaking through.' I said: 'No. This has got to be just the wall, because I am talking about resistance as obduracy, as well

as talking about it literally as the concrete physical wall
snaking through the territory.' In the end he agreed, and
allowed the poster for my lecture to be just the wall, but
the poster for the conference to be his picture of the wall
with the Palestinian clambering over it. So we made a
happy compromise. Resistance at that level is also crucial,
and the Palestinian resistance—since it is one of the
longest-running occupations in history—has today, it could
be said, a right to the title 'The Last Resistance' for itself.
However—and this is where Said is very important—resistance must not transmute itself into a rigid self-given form
of political identity. He was so clear about that, as, I think,
was Mahmoud Darwish in his poetry. If there is to be
Palestinian national identity, it mustn't be like all the other
national identities. Resistance as political struggle must not
become resistance in the bad psychic sense once you've
achieved your aims. There *has* to be a contrapuntal form of
identity. You have to use music—and this would be dear to
your heart, Aveek—to modulate the potential rigidity of
identity. Otherwise, you end up with the last resistance in
the bad sense. I am really interested in the connection
between these two. To say something much more simple:
for me, what's interesting is the relationship between the
psychic and the political, and the struggles in both
domains, how they inform each other, relate to each
other. When I am talking about politics, I am always look-

ing over my shoulder, if you like, to see the psychic components of this struggle, to see what is being played out here psychically and politically. What's going to emerge? Are identities going to harden into place in which case there will not be 'suffering enough for everybody', or are they going to ease up or open up in some way?

SC. In the case of the suicide bomber, would you say that obviously, here, there is the very coercive role of the superego imposing a code of conduct to a political end which is also a psychic end? But, at the same time, if you think of Freud's wonderful essay on one's attitude to death, and try to bring that into our thoughts about the suicide bomber: there is a great deal of resistance to be overcome in order to appear as the model of the 'resistance fighter'. So, to *be* the resistance fighter, you have to overcome all kinds of resistance within yourself, and that can only be done in a very coercive personal mode. You have written about this.

JR. Well, this is a very tricky topic. I don't know if you've seen the film *Paradise Now*[9] . . .

SC. No.

JR. It is an extraordinary Palestinian film about two suicide bombers, their training and their relationship with their families, and the consequences of the failure of their mission at the start of the film. I show it at the end of a course I am teaching on Palestinian–Israeli fiction at London University, and the students are so distressed by it because they know they are being asked to understand the mind, the history, the family of a suicide bomber. Even though at moments there is comedy. There is also a very strong scene of dialogue in a car between a Palestinian woman, the daughter of a hero of the resistance, who's come back to her village for the first time, and one of the boys who is planning a suicide-bombing mission, who is the son of somebody who was killed as a collaborator. She attacks suicide bombing as futile and self-defeating and he defends it. So these suicide bombers have their psychic history. We see the different positions from which they come. There is a link here to Eyad El-Sarraj, who runs the Gaza Mental Health Programme, who has repeatedly said that the generation of the second Intifada has been violent in a way that the first was not, because these are the nineteen- and twenty-year-old sons of fathers who were humiliated in the first Intifada. Therefore, this is about father–son relationships and the degradation of the Palestinian people, which I think is not stressed enough. It's not just that they are a defeated people who have been deprived of their land and sovereignty and of a nation-state; it's also that they are degraded people, on a daily basis. And I think this played an important part in the violence of the second Intifada and in the recourse to violence by some Palestinians more generally.

But behind what you're saying, there's another very difficult question which I'm not sure if I'm qualified to answer, about different cultures' attitude to death. When I was thinking about suicide bombing, I really wanted to avoid what I saw as the trap of saying that of course Palestinians are a culture of death, which is so often said, that they value death, and we, meaning the West and Israel, value life. I find that sinister and so wrong. This also becomes very complex. So, for example, there is a huge distinction in Islam as I understand it, between suicide and martyrdom. Calling these people suicide bombers is to degrade them. Suicide is a personal act, and it's against the will of God, and hence a sin in the Qur'an. But martyrdom is something else. And, you know, martyrdom has a lengthy Christian tradition, to say the least. I start the essay on suicide bombing by talking about *Anna Karenina* [1878] and the moment near the end of the novel where Vronsky, on his way to the front, knows that he is going to kill soldiers and wants to die in that moment. So, he is, in a sense, a suicide bomber, or a martyr. He wants to die and kill in the same breath. That book is one of the classics of European culture. And, as has also been pointed out by others, Samson can be seen as the first great suicide bomber. Samson is a Zionist hero. Jabotinsky, one of the most influential Zionist thinkers and the founder of Revisionist Zionism, wrote one of his novels about Samson.[10] So I feel I am treading on broken glass in this area, because you are called upon to make generalizations about Palestinian culture, religion and thought, which I feel I'm not qualified to make. Even if I were, I wouldn't want to make them.

SC. Yes, but political murder is very likely to involve one's death, even if one is not a suicide bomber in the practical sense of not having the explosives strapped to your body. This has become fairly common in the subcontinent. I am sure you know that Rajiv Gandhi was killed by a suicide bomber. Benazir Bhutto—I was at Oxford with her—was killed by a suicide bomber . . .

JR. Can I interrupt you there? Isn't there a dispute now that she might not have been killed with a laser gun?

SC. Right, that is the latest theory. Anyway, at the same time, anybody who takes the risk in a public place of shooting somebody with a gun is very likely to be killed immediately. That is pretty close to being a suicide assassin. And martyrdom obviously is part of the deal for the person who is thus convinced of the need to do so.

JR. There's something else here that confuses me. I do not understand why it is seen as ethically superior to drop bombs from a plane rather than to go to a market and blow yourself up as well as your victim. For some reason, suicide bombing evokes that kind of revulsion and a special form of ethical judgement. For me, it is a crime. I have no desire to support or justify suicide bombing, and I want to make it clear that the killing of civilians is unjustified under any circumstances. But, for some reason, this is seen as the worst form of killing, worse than, say, the bombing of a country from the air where you then fly away. Something I was trying to probe in the essay was why this is felt to be so uniquely horrific. I concluded that there was something about the intimacy. Suicide bombing is a deadly embrace. It's a form of contact. Both David Grossman and Amos Oz have written about the hideous intimacy of war—bodies start to tear and merge, and people get caught up with each other in ways that are horrendously close. One of the frightening things about modern warfare is the fantasy that America has now: of a war in which there would be no casualties on the American side, no body bags, the vision of the smart bomb. It is a fantasy of a war in which your body is completely unharmed. There is something very strange going on, which raises a psychoanalytic question.

AS. It is really about the separation of the weapon from the body, as it were, and therefore, a kind of letting-go of responsibility. Do you think . . . ?

JR. Say some more, Aveek . . .

SC. Yes, please go on, and then I would like to comment . . .

AS. Because the suicide bomber's weapons are strapped to the body, whereas modern war technology is moving the weapons further and further away, and the targets further and further away . . .

JR. So the body doesn't feel contaminated in some sense. So you can feel pure. You can feel unmarked by the violence.

AS. Yes!

JR. You feel unmarked by the violence you are carrying out against the Other.

SC. That's one possibility. Another possibility that strikes me is that the person who has murdered from a distance is seen as having chosen life rather than death for himself or herself. And that again is very crippling—and that's why I reread Freud's 'On Our Attitude to Death'[11]—to think that anyone would choose death. So long as they haven't chosen death, they can be as brutal and as terrible a soldier as they wish to be.

JR. Yes, I agree with you. One of the best moments in that wonderful essay is when he describes the warriors returning from war, and how they sit outside the tribe and grieve for the people that they have killed. He is talking about what he calls 'primitive' cultures—a problematic term, to say the least, that he uses with regularity—but this is an instance where the West comes off very badly by comparison. He is saying that in those cultures you cannot detach yourself from the violence that you have committed—you have to reincorporate it in some way. So, this idea of 'I have chosen life'—I choose life at any cost—when you've just killed a thousand people with impunity doesn't strike me as particularly impressive.

SC. It's not impressive.

JR. Two other things that I think are important in this. I was at a film conference to mark a year after 9/11. Apparently, footage of the bodies falling from the buildings, aired immediately after, was then pulled from US television. After the first day, that footage was never seen again, until it was revived and became an object of discussion, part of a debate as a particular filmic, and historical, moment. A professor from Pittsburg argued that, in American culture, bodies must not be seen to die. You have life and you have death, but you must not see the transition, death happening, because it confronts the Americans with a mortality that the culture is geared to refusing. For Walter Benjamin, the writer used to take his authority from death—there would not be a room in which somebody hadn't died—but now we push it away to the outskirts and margins of the culture. We are touching here on very difficult questions: about how different cultures relate in a more integrated way perhaps—certainly more than the way Western culture would, which is the only one I can speak for—to the question of death.

This also relates to our discussion on identification, because even our conversation here about suicide bombers would be considered by some people to be out of line. So, when Cherie Blair, in one of her better moments—I'm not a fan—said she might do the same if she were leading such a despairing life, Downing Street apologized. When Jenny Tonge, a Liberal Democrat front-bench spokesperson, said something similar, she was immediately sacked from the front bench of her party. It's as if you must not claim to understand or empathize—if you do either you are condoning. One of the points of writing about this, then, is to say that to understand is not to condone the act. It is to ask under what conditions any of us might behave in a certain way. It is to try and universalize the predicament. Even Ehud Barak said that if he were a Palestinian, he'd be a suicide bomber.

AS. So would you not accept the limits that Coetzee puts in *Elizabeth Costello* [2003], for instance, to the whole question of imagining oneself into evil?

JR. This is Coetzee's extraordinary essay on evil you are referring to, which I had the privilege of hearing him read for the first time in Amsterdam at the Nexus Institute in a conference on evil. Coetzee clearly made it a condition of attending the conference, where we were all expected to read formal papers on the question, that he would only come if he could read a piece that would be a fictional rendering of Elizabeth Costello arriving at a conference on evil, picking up Elizabeth Costello from what at that time was just 'The Lives of Animals', a character from the Tanner lectures he had delivered at Princeton. Costello's topic is *The Very Rich Hours of Count von Stauffenberg* [Paul West, 1989], which describes the execution of Hitler's would-be assassins. In the course of the book, the narrator, who turns out to be sitting in the audience as she speaks, imagines himself in the position of the would-be 'assassins' of Hitler in their very last moments. Coetzee, or rather Costello, says that this is going too far, that we should not imagine ourselves in such a moment, above all that the writer should not enter moments of pure evil—to do so is to risk making evil attractive, tempting. I felt myself in total disagreement with him for a number of reasons. One, in order to make his argument work, we had to identify with Elizabeth Costello being repelled by this moment. Furthermore, in the course of her talk, she remembers a scene of sexual violence to which she was subjected as a young woman and which is described in graphic detail. Listening was a really strange experience. There was Coetzee, a man, speaking in the voice of a woman about a female sexual experience of horrendous violence, which we were being required to identify with in order to understand why this other book shouldn't have been written because it asks you for one identification too many, or too far. So, it's self-defeating. The more successfully or fully we identified with Elizabeth Costello in order to enter into her argument, the more we were doing the very thing that she was arguing was too dangerous to do.

Let's be fair to Coetzee: I'm sure he knew exactly what he was doing, and therefore the book, the lecture, was rehearsing the dilemma it described. On the other hand, if I did have an ethical objection, it's because it's very important in *Disgrace* [1999] that Lucy, when she has been raped, never talks to her father, David Lurie, about what has happened, and that he is brought to recognize that there are some places where he knows he cannot go. That is, Coetzee in that book draws a line, a limit to identification. A man cannot imagine himself in the place of a female rape victim. It's as if in the Elizabeth Costello lecture, Coetzee had decided he was going to do just that. I felt he'd slightly betrayed his own feminist point. If I am being consistent, however, then he should be allowed to do it, because the point of reading fiction is that you become somebody else, or it doesn't work. Therefore all fiction in a sense requires us to step over a boundary that is obscene, that is off-stage to us, that we are allowed, or required, to identify with. This is a fundamental question about the limits and temptations of literary identification. We all know how this works. Coetzee's piece is finally brilliant for showing how the problem of identifying with evil is simply an inflated version of what it means to read fiction at all. So, I disagreed with the manifest content of his utterance but I agree with its latent performance.

AS. Can I shift the discussion a bit? I want to come back to your brilliant lecture yesterday.[12] It not only gave us wonderful ideas and analyses, but also a set of very beautiful images. And there is one I want to dwell on a bit—the image of the house with the moving walls. And I want to just relocate the image a bit and ask you about the house of your intellectual being. How do the walls move there? What kind of journeys has taken you from Peter Pan to Palestine, from Psychoanalysis to Literature? I noticed that,

in the course of this discussion, you seem to move effortlessly from the death of your sister to talking about nation-
states. Could you tell us about these movements of the
walls?

JR. Well, it's very difficult to talk about oneself at that
level of self-consciousness because these things sort of
happen. And effortlessly, I would say, is not quite the right
word for me. To go right back to the beginning of this
conversation, you find your interests mutating and shifting in response to the exigencies of the here and the now.
But there are real continuities. I need to go back to
Sexuality in the Field of Vision, which argued that feminism
needed psychoanalysis. I'm very indebted to Juliet
Mitchell, of course, with whom I translated Lacan's texts on
femininity a quarter of a century ago. (I love saying that: 'a
quarter of a century ago'.) What we both felt then, and
what Mitchell's brilliant *Psychoanalysis and Feminism* had
said—it had a profound political effect in 1973 when it
came out in England—is that you can't have an account
of femininity as simply patriarchal social mapping onto
the body of the woman. Obviously, you can't have a bio-
logically determinist account—that women are born
women—that would be reactionary. We need something
which explains how 'becoming a woman' enters into the
mind and body in the most subtle, complex, sometimes

self-defeating, sometimes creative, intractable ways. This was a political problem, as she also wanted psychoanalysis to be part of political discourse in response to the feeling that the bullyboys of the Marxist Left (to put it very simply; I'm not sure she would use that expression) were not attuned to the importance of fantasy life in the constitution of political identities. They were not interested in sexuality either, which is to say the same thing. There was also a recognition that the Right knows how to mobilize sexual fantasy and identity—fascism, for example, with its symbols, marches and uniforms, and its euphoria and sexualized excitement—in the way that the Left tragically has never managed to do. Not that the Left would want to do it in that way, but it's left the field of the psychosexual open to the opposition. So, that was the atmosphere then. My feminism was very much to do with trying to wed the psychic and the political in some way.

But it was also a critique of the radical feminist argument: that all men are the enemies of all women, which also implies that all men are—to the minutest core of their identity, an identity they fulfil in every moment— men. I think there is a big problem here. What I love about psychoanalysis is that it says that our identities are precariously sustained. If we want to draw on that insight and say, for women, that there is an inner vacillation, that we are not the stereotype that the culture wishes us to be, that we are more than that, then how can we not say the same thing about men also? How can we not give them the same margin to free themselves from that rigidity of an identification we, as feminists, diagnose as so pernicious? Obviously, you can argue that there is an important asymmetry—that the social advantages lie with such a blind espousal of male identity. But psychoanalysis believes, as I have already said today, that there is no identity without fissure, and that the more rigidly you hold on to an identity, the higher the psychic price. It seems to me we should be preserving that insight in order to prise apart—or, rather, to show as untenable—the worst of what patriarchy requires men to be. In teaching feminism, I always say that if patriarchal ideology were not effective, we would not need feminism. But if it were one hundred per cent effective, then we would not have feminism. So, there's a break in the system, or there would be no transformation. Psychoanalysis and feminism were therefore crucial for me together.

Psychoanalysis was also urgent because it stops you from being a victim by making you the psychic agent of your own life which becomes available—not easily, but through a process of internal struggle—for transformation. You're never therefore simply a woman—you're more complex than that. And your story has never been definitively told. Those are two political insights which I think we need. Now, in a sense, the work on Israel–Palestine is the logical extension of the same thing. There is a strand of feminism and a strand of Zionism, which have in common the claim for a monopoly of suffering. At moments, the same psychic thread weaves through them both.

There's also the crucial question of Judaism. As my mother would testify—she is sitting in the audience, and I am delighted to have her here this evening—I was brought up in an atmosphere where the Jewish religion was seen, as it had been for her, as predominantly oppressive to women, hostile to the educational possibilities of my mother, in particular, who was not allowed by her parents to take up a place she had won at medical school—her lifelong dream. And, understandably, as also defensive. My maternal grandmother got out of Poland just in time; the rest of the family were sent to Chelmno. This led to a very rigid, uncreative Jewish identity. In my family life, it was based on observance. There was no sense of a Judaism rooted in compassion or justice, the very different strand of Judaism which I have spent the last ten to twenty years or so discovering. So part of what I have been doing is to try and understand what could be thought creatively about Judaism. As I say in the piece about Gillian, at a time when the three of us were not particularly in touch with each other, she was writing on Holocaust theology and the work of Emile Fackenheim; Braham, our first cousin, was doing a Holocaust production of *Macbeth*, which he staged in a concentration camp—we know that inmates did perform, Verdi's *Requiem* for example, but by staging *Macbeth* they were performing the genesis of evil on their own behalf; I was working on the place of the Holocaust in the poetry of Sylvia Plath, which led me to try to understand the Holocaust through reading for the first time. We were all doing this at a time when we did not know that the other was also involved in the same task. We might call it, to modify Freud, a 'return of the political repressed'. A history that had been too painful to talk about in my family was bubbling up to the surface and becoming something we each felt the need, separately but in some strange connected way, to think about.

So, two things sort of shifted and mutated together: the idea of a political discourse that would not be rigid and would refuse the category of the victim and a monopoly of suffering, and the need to acknowledge a history of suffering at the same time. You might see how those two things start to come together and then collide.

In the dominant discourse, if you acknowledge Israel's suffering or the suffering of the Jewish people, then you do not critique state power. If you critique state power, then you have to silence the question of the suffering of the Jewish people. I wanted a vocabulary and a discourse where you say both those things at the same time. And that leads back to Plath. For me, the wonder of Plath is that, in the space of a line of poetry, she can rail against patriarchal figures—you know, fathers, husbands, doctors— and lament or even celebrate her passionate attachment for them at the same time. That is, she knows that the political reproach does not exhaust the internal, psychic options. The psychic complexity and the cry against injustice are there together in the same line—you don't even have to turn the page, let alone go to a different poem or piece of writing, and definitely not to another writer, to find all of that at once.

The image of the 'moving walls' is, therefore, an attempt to stretch the contours of our being to get these things together, or, rather, in order to be able to see that they are already there. It's like that eye test we had as children in England—nothing like the one I had today, by the way, in Calcutta—where you had to get the lion into the cage, even though they were not, or seemed not to be, quite in the same dimension. If you couldn't do it, it meant there was something wrong with your eyesight. Well, I love the idea that there is something fundamentally wrong with my eyesight, or, rather, that we need to see the world through this slightly disjointed, incompatible prism.

SC. So, the term, perhaps, that we need to remind ourselves of is 'literature', obviously. It's literature that takes these risks and that can say two things at the same time. 'Kill and not kill': I think that's in another essay of yours. So, the possibility of imagining two completely contrary things at the same time is obviously there in literature.

AS. You have written fiction too. What was the unthinkable there? And you have gone back to Proust . . .

JR. *Albertine* [2001] was stimulated by one moment in *A la recherche*, the end of which centres on him trapping in his Paris apartment the beautiful orphan Albertine. He was about to dump her, but, as they are driving home in the carriage from Madame Verdurin's, Albertine confesses that she knew a woman, a friend of a woman who, four volumes earlier, the narrator had seen having lesbian sex through a window. In fact, they close the curtains before they did, but it's clear that's what they're going to do. The thought that Albertine might be a lesbian immediately leads him to fall back in love with her, and to take

her to Paris and lock her up in the apartment. This is why
Proust, as far as I'm concerned, is one step ahead of
Freud in terms of the vicarious perversion of human
desire. You might think he would have lost all interest in
her whatsoever, but the opposite is true. Anyway, he more
or less traps her in the apartment. And she's complicit
with it—she's not completely against it. She wants the
power and she wants to rise up the social hierarchy. She
also wants to be free, but there is a more complex attachment between them. The crucial scene for me comes
when Albertine is asleep, and the narrator comes into the
room, lies down beside her, and 'embarks on the boat of
her sleep'—it is one of the most beautiful passages in the
whole book—up to and including the fact that he mastur-
bates against her body. I am a feminist, but the particular
form of feminist reaction I had in response to this scene
is not typical for me. I just sat up and thought, she is not
asleep! No woman would sleep through this! This is the
most unrealistic, unacceptable, moment in the whole
thing (I am not normally into lifting women as characters
off the page but in seeing how they are held within it).
So, I decided I wanted to write a novel from Albertine's
point of view. At one point, the narrator says: 'The pages
I would write, Albertine would certainly not have understood. Had she been capable of understanding them, she

would, for that very reason, not have inspired them.' This is the epigraph to the novel. The whole point of the novel was to circulate back to that one scene, and to write it with her awake.

Writing the novel has changed the way I teach. Now when I read fiction, I'm not just looking to see what happens or how I am being drawn in or what is the thought behind the scene. I am, for example, looking to see how many times the writer can get the word 'but' into one paragraph, or how many similes are there on one page— I have become much more interested in the technical process of how you can create or craft a scene, in what you can do and not do with language, what works and doesn't work, although most often you cannot answer why. It has been like educating myself from scratch all over again.

AS. You were talking about the way writing a novel has changed the way you teach, and your students figure very prominently in your writing. What is the relationship, in your career, between teaching and psychoanalysis? I am referring particularly to the way you read Christopher Bollas about the Unconscious of two people rubbing against one another in the analytic setting. Does that happen in teaching?

JR. It's a very strange process. Gillian once said that in order to teach, you have to ignore ninety per cent of what's going on in the room, but then when you get home at night that ninety per cent hits you between the eyes—because you can't actually pay attention to all the psychic dynamics in the room without abusing privacy, and because you see things which you shouldn't always be seeing. Teaching psychoanalysis is a very strange thing to do. There are three levels of language. There's the language we are using now. There's the language of the Unconscious—let's call it the language of dreams. And there's metalanguage, which is language about language. When you're in a seminar on literature or psychoanalysis, you're using metalanguage, which is language about language. The Unconscious is on the third, lower, mostly hidden level, and the language of the seminar is at the highest formal level. It's not even on the middle. So, how do you access the Unconscious? How can you get to it? Of course, you can't. That is the terrible problem I always have about teaching psychoanalysis, which is that even if your propositions are clear—for instance, the proposition that 'Everyone knows if he or she is a man or a woman, but the Unconscious knows better' might work as a proposition—but in relation to what it is trying to evoke, in relation to the Unconscious, it's a corrupt statement because it is too formal, too elevated and far from its object as we might say. This is true of all teaching to some extent but it is particularly acute in teaching psychoanalysis. You can of course do so—there is a Freudian theory that can, and I think, still today or even more today, needs to be taught. But that is only half the story. That is one reason why I so often teach psychoanalysis with literature, or with politics, in order to dislodge the purity of the language being used to describe it. One of the courses I most love teaching is a course on Freud and Proust, where we read, say, Freud's 'Disturbance of Memory on the Acropolis' [1936] and then the Madeleine episode from Proust, not to make one apply to the other but just to notice how, in both passages or forms of writing, something about memory and subjectivity is disintegrating on the page. It is an attempt to produce moments of writing which mimic something of the process of unconscious thought, which is where literature becomes so crucial again.

Occasionally, in relation to psychoanalysis, the lines between the different levels of language are breached. When, for example, a student thinks he or she can turn the seminar experience of psychoanalysis into something very personal. You have to redraw a line there. Very rigidly. This is a boundary which touches on the professional ethics of teaching. You have to know when to suggest to a student that they instead see a counsellor or find another space. At the same time, you have to be very careful because the normal issues of transference, which are present in all teaching, can be intensified when you are teaching psychoanalysis. Shoshana Felman has written brilliantly about trying to find a form of teaching in which you abrogate your power, give it up in some sense, avoid the pitfall of acting counter-transferentially without fail. In her own practice, she tries to produce a model for such teaching. I personally think the problem is impossible to solve.

sc. In your writing, have you felt that you are no longer using so much psychoanalysis as a mode of explanation—it never was one anyway—and that you are moving away from that position to thinking of not just one analogy but many kinds of analogies through which looking at psychoanalysis or thinking in terms of psychoanalysis becomes illuminating? It's not a way of explaining things. It's a way of just casting a reflection . . .

jr. That's so interesting. The central chapter in the book on Zionism [*The Question of Zion*, 2005]—'Zionism as Psychoanalysis'—is about all those thinkers I have mentioned this evening, who I think had psychoanalytic insights about the underside of an official Zionist rhetoric. This is not explicit in their writing of course, but without psychoanalysis casting an oblique reflection on their thought, I do not think I would have been able to grasp the full import of their critique. It is that idea of obliqueness that I think I most often lift from psychoanalysis. On the course I teach on the Israeli–Palestinian conflict, we read Chaim Weizmann, Theodor Herzl and David Ben-Gurion, the founding fathers. But we also read the fiction, starting with Yehuda Amichai and Mahmoud Darwish. They become each other's uninvited commentators. It is the literature that gives the students hope. Because much as I am an admirer of Jacques Derrida and the possibility of deconstructing any statement, when Chaim Weizmann says of Palestine that it will be 'as England is English', or that they will go there 'whether the Arabs want it or not', I defy anybody to deconstruct those statements. There is nothing you can do with them. The fiction, on the other hand, knows what the political rhetoric cannot bear to hear. So I am setting up a kind of psychoanalytic dialogue between the fiction and the dominant discourse.

But you're right in another way. The only way to read Freud is as someone struggling with thought. I would be lying if I didn't admit to undergraduates that there are certain concepts I want them to come away with: the Unconscious, bisexuality, the shift in Freud's understanding of femininity. That is also a pedagogic imperative.

But, at the same time, I always encourage students to listen, hold on, to the questions Freud is asking. Even when they don't like his answers—and he is surely not at his best when he thinks he has the answers—they might continue to respect the question. So, it is, yes, finally a speculative way of working with Freud.

SC. There were a couple of questions that I didn't manage to ask. I'll just mention them. You don't necessarily have to comment on both. We didn't really talk a great deal about partition, and I had thought that we would. And I had some questions about the land and body and even that phrase that is now very common in journalism, the position of an 'embedded' journalist, the 'embeddedness'—the idea of the place as an extension of the body, and what this means for a land that is divided and people who are forced to relocate. That's one area we might have thought about. And the other—we didn't discuss your work on the cinema, and I really wanted to.

JR. The cinema is a long time ago. So I am not going to try that one, except to say that it was through film theory that psychoanalysis, in its Freud–Lacan axis, entered cultural discourse in England in the Seventies so that psychoanalysis was linked, from early on, to the question of how images are constituted and their power. That was the decisive link to feminism, specifically to the feminist question I discussed earlier—of how femininity entrenches itself in, or seduces, the mind—which is where the psychoanalysis-and-feminism dialogue began.

But in relationship to the land, I agree. In his book *The Third Way* [1982], Rajeh Shehadeh, the amazing human rights lawyer, and writer, from Ramallah, talks of a 'pornography of the land', which influenced me greatly in thinking about the conflict. He is describing the over-investment in and sacralization of the land in Zionism. This is a real problem for Judaism in relation to what has happened in Israel, because, in the Bible, God instructs Abraham to move and to go towards a land, but it is a notion of a voice and of a certain kind of movement which is necessarily above the land to which it only obliquely refers. In his brilliant article 'The Double Site of Israel',[13] the Israeli writer Zvi Gurevitch argues that there are two different notions of the land in Jewish thinking. The biblical one is the land as the place where God is present, but also crucially not present. And the political one is land as something that can be conquered. So if you are true to the religious conception of the land, you do not own it and never can because God is an invisible presence and can never be concretized. It is a form of ideology—the famous Israeli dissident Yeshayahu

Leibowitz called it idolatry—to sacralize the land as possession. This brings us back to the intellectual godfather of Hindutva, quoted by Tharoor, for whom the fatherland as land was holy. We need to unpack these forms of investment. Nadine Gordimer once wrote that the only valid attachment to the land is attachment to the people: 'You cannot be "attached" to soil and thorn trees, because these do not respond.'[14] You can belong to the land, you can even feel that it holds the traces of your ancestral belonging, but to fetishize it is a category mistake.

In Zionism, in fact, the debate about the land is complex. I'd be interested to know how you see the analogies. Weizmann for one believed that the claim to the land had to be built up bit by bit through work; Ben-Gurion said that the Bible is our mandate. These are two very different ways of laying claim to the land. The vision of the land is contested inside Zionism, although even the notion of entitlement through labour of course simply ignores the fact that there were other people— Palestinians—on the land who were indeed working it. So none of these concepts are free of contamination. But I'd love to hear more from you about how these ideas are working in terms of Partition in India and Pakistan.

sc. Well, in Bengal particularly I think that it's not a question of sacralizing the land, not a question of laying possession in terms of a holy mandate or a holy prescription. It's more a deep problem of belonging to certain places from which very large populations have been dislocated over a period of time. Partition was one moment—1947— but it happened earlier also. It was just a repetition of something that had already taken place. The British had already divided Bengal in 1905–06, and that was the occasion for bitter protest and resistance. Subsequently, you can't even think of 1947 as a dividing line, because people were moving across the border and continue to move to this day to find a resting place for themselves. I recently translated a section from a wonderful memoir by Shanta Sen called *Grandmother* (*Pitamahi*; [1994]), where she is talking actually about her own grandmother, who, at a very late stage (in 1950), decides to leave her ancestral village in East Bengal and come to the West. It's already very late, too late. The others are gone. She is an old woman, over seventy, I think, possibly eighty, and she crosses with a group of people. It's a very terrible debilitating journey, and she dies at the end of it. She says goodbye to her home in a very formal, very correct, way. So it's not that she owns the land, or possesses it. She *can* leave it. But it causes pain. That's the point, really.

JR. So, she's leaving her ancestral home in the East to come to the West . . .

sc. Yes. This is post Partition. Other people have already left. She is one of the countless refugees who leave *after* 1947.

jr. This sounds extraordinary—it seems as if she has this internal mobility that is accompanying her actual external journey. Whereas, of course, what has emerged in the response to the *nakba* or catastrophe of 1948 for the Palestinians—and you can see this most strongly in Darwish's poetry—is a discourse of yearning and of longing with no possible remission. Many Palestinians still have the keys to their original houses. One of the tragedies of this conflict is that there are two concepts of belonging contesting each other. The Zionist claim is that 'This was our kingdom two thousand years ago, therefore it is our ancestral home'—although whether or in what form that was true is now the object of debate. Interestingly, Herzl himself supported the Ugandan option, but it was defeated because, in Ben-Gurion's words, Palestine was the only land for which the Jewish people would be 'willing to suffer'. Suffering was therefore inscribed into Zionist identity, not just as memory but as a kind of obligation. Against this is the idea of belonging based on a far more immediate sense of past history and entitlement, and on being there now, which is closer to the Palestinian claim. When I was making the film

Dangerous Liaison—Israel and America, for Channel 4
Television in 2002, Najey Gazouna, a Palestinian from
Ramallah, pointed to where his grandparents are buried.
This is where he belonged. On both sides of this conflict,
the notion of what it means to belong is becoming more
and more fixed, although with very different emphases
and political consequences—crucially, there is no symme-
try; Israel is the occupying power—on each side. And, in
both cases, it is a discourse of mourning, a mourning that
refuses to be mourning because the thing that has been
lost must be repossessed. It's as if the land has become a
ghostly territory crying out to be re-inhabited. Whereas in
the memoir you've just described, it sounds as if she was
living out the problem of what it meant to move, and what
it would do, although it seems fatally in the end, to her.

SC. I think both Aveek and I come from families which
moved, which crossed the border and relocated from East
Bengal to the West. So, we come from families of
refugees. But India is full of refugees. So are Pakistan and
Bangladesh. This is a subcontinent whose populations
have moved so many times, are still moving. The borders
are still not fixed, not completely determined. There is
still a migrant population which crosses for reasons of
trade or economic betterment and sometimes makes their
pile and goes back.

JR. This now becomes even more complex, doesn't it? Because the idea of the migration of peoples is sometimes seen as one of the most creative aspects of modern times. At the same time, it can be seen as the worst aspect, the creation of stateless people and refugees as the necessary accompaniment to the formation of modern nation-states. And it can also be seen as global capital just simply moving people, as disposable goods, around the world according to where the labour is cheap and so on. So this is an example where the idea of mutability has to be unpacked both for its creative and destructive components.

AS. Yes, because Partition is not just expelling, but is also accommodation. And deeply ambivalent accommodation. It's very interesting that the places, the neighbourhoods, created by settled refugees are called 'colonies', which have now become part of greater Calcutta . . .

JR. Why were they called colonies?

SC. It was a British term. You know, like Defence Colony, Bagha Jatin Colony: 'colony' as a settlement of people, like colonies of ants. This is just, you know . . .

AS. A coincidence . . .

SC. A coincidence. But, you know, there's a colonial and postcolonial history of India that has not been told, and I am always urging research students to look at this, because we need to look at the history of the colony in that sense: the settlement of migrated people, the people who have shifted from . . .

JR. But it sounds as if what you're describing is something positive in a way, as creating genuine new communities?

SC. But founded on suffering and dispossession. And very poor people. Endurance. A great deal of suffering. Constant battles fought with the authorities. These are often illegal shanty towns.

JR. Ah, I misunderstood you . . .

SC. And another thing perhaps one could mention. The modern Indian novelist Amitav Ghosh, several of whose novels have to do with Partition, deals with this history in many ways; not only in *Shadow Lines* [1990], which is about Calcutta and Dhaka and the consequences of the Partition, but also in a recent novel, *The Hungry Tide* [2004], where he talks about the Sunderbans, the deltaic region close to Calcutta, the mouth of the Ganges. And there, very interestingly, he is also talking about the kind of sedimentation of history and of settlement, which has to contend not only with political expulsion and political relocation but also with ecology, with Nature, with devastation caused by natural disasters. And if you look at the recent history of Bangladesh and India, then you have to think of environmental refugees and settlements and all the problems that are associated with these. And a third element to bring into this is the recent violence in a place called Nandigram, not very far from Calcutta, where economic improvement—

AS. Industrialization—

SC. Industrialization is creating a new category of refugees and displaced persons.

JR. Now I have understood you more clearly. All these have to do with displacements in the sense of human vulnerability, either expulsion or statelessness or refugee status. These all sound like the detritus of a ruthless global economy and a set of political decisions over which the people most profoundly affected have no say. When you were talking, of course, and using the word 'settlement' over and over again, what was ringing in my mind were the settlements in the occupied territories in Israel–Palestine. Although the question as to whether the occupation is illegal can be debated in international law, what is unequivocally illegal is the transfer of population—I am not referring here to the expulsion of the Palestinians—but the transfer of Israeli citizens into the occupied territory. International law bars the settlement of people into what is meant to be a temporary situation. In that sense, we are talking about settlements as literally the blot on the face of the landscape, and the major obstruction to any form of satisfactory peace solution in Israel–Palestine. As we speak, when the Annapolis Conference was going on—a complete waste of space, as I see it—permissions were being granted for three hundred more homes to be built in East Jerusalem. So, I was thinking of 'settlement' in that negative sense. I think what you're talking about is the extent to which our world is an offspring of a set of historical mutations, which are interminable in some sense, and which, as Arundhati Roy stresses, are creating a new set of historic injustices on the ground.

QUESTION 1. Can I ask something [. . .] about the English language? Obama just won an election in America, and he has promised Americans that he is going to control outsourcing. For Indians, especially young urban Indians—the new generation—outsourced jobs are an important source of income. But at the same time, in the US or the UK, people are losing jobs and hence protesting against the practice of outsourcing. As a teacher and a humanist, what do you think about this? Could Indians at large do anything to solve this problem?

JR. I was very struck reading the papers this morning and very glad to be reading about Obama's victory here. He is a Black American—he might be the first Black President of America—and yet he promised never to outsource to India and China. This might be seen as feeding on a form of American patriotic, potentially racist, national-ism, although I prefer to think not, and, given his history, this seems unlikely. But it reminded me of Gordon Brown's—the UK's Prime Minister's—speech at the Labour Party Conference a few months ago where he talked about 'British jobs for British workers'. Anybody vaguely on the Left of British politics was horrified because these are words that could have could have come out of the mouth of the National Front [Britain's racist proto-fascist party]. So obviously, outsourcing involves the exploitation of cheap overseas labour. In England, there has been a big scandal over stores such as Primark and H&M—Primark, the low-cost clothing outlet, was the worst. It turned out these very cheap clothes which every-one was queuing up to buy had been produced by out-sourced labour paid at sometimes five pence an hour, which is about fifteen rupees. So, outsourcing should stop. Not because Americans should have the jobs rather than people overseas, but in terms of a decent living wage. There is currently a big campaign going on in

England to make sure that these companies are watched, to make them accountable so they are obliged to ensure that their labour is paid a living wage, but how successful that's going to be is not clear. This is a wonderful example of split political rhetoric, in which the question of 'what is the right way to jump?' is at once clear and complex. I'd love to hear from Supriya and Aveek on this.

SC. Actually I agree with you on outsourcing. I mean, I can see that it is split down the middle in terms of exploiting poor people, but, on the other hand, providing opportunities for work to people who might not otherwise have those opportunities. I think what we need is to think ourselves—China, India and other Asian countries. We need to do the thinking on this. It is not for the West to decide whether they would outsource or not. It's for us to decide whether we want to be primarily a slave economy or whether we want to produce things for ourselves, which are perhaps better than those the West produces. So, I think here it's very much a question of self-definition, as it were, not in terms of a decision taken in the West about outsourcing or not outsourcing.

QUESTION 2. This relates to a problem you discussed very early in the conversation: the Truth and Reconciliation Commission. How viable is it to use in the Palestinian conflict—because isn't one country's terrorist another country's freedom fighter?

JR. Before he died, Edward Said wanted there to be a Truth and Reconciliation Commission in Israel–Palestine, partly as a way of determining what version of history should be taught in schools, to establish the truth of 1948. There is at present a massive split between the new historians, such as Avi Shlaim, Tom Segev and Ilan Pappé, and the old Zionist historians whose narrative was an uncritical apology for Israel. At a Conference of the Faculty for Israeli–Palestine Peace in 2006, Gillian Slovo, daughter of Joe Slovo and Ruth First, now a distinguished novelist who was brought from South Africa to live in exile in Britain as a child, argued that you cannot have truth and reconciliation until you have justice. In South Africa, apartheid ended and then you had the Truth and Reconciliation Commission. I found that very moving, and convincing. Thank you.

SC. Thank you for that question. That brings us back to the question of how you define justice without a notion of truth. And that brings us back to the beginning, and, you know, we could start this conversation all over again. But thank you very much, Jacqueline, for a wonderful discussion. And I think Aveek would like to add his thanks to mine.

AS. Yes, and as you have written about psychoanalysis, there can be and must be no last word. But we all have to finish here and I would certainly like to say thank you for yesterday and today and to Supriya for being here and joining this conversation.

JR. Thank you both very much. It's been a wonderful conversation, a real dialogue, rather than anything else. I've much appreciated your thoughts. I am at least as grateful to you as the other way around. So thank you to the audience as well.

SUPRIYA CHAUDHURI is Professor of English at Jadavpur University, Calcutta. AVEEK SEN is Senior Assistant Editor, Editorial Pages, *The Telegraph*, Calcutta.

Notes

1 Jacqueline Rose, 'On Gillian Rose', in *The Last Resistance* (London: Verso, 2007), pp. 223–30.

2 Both books were made available in a paperback edition for India and the subcontinent by Seagull Books, Calcutta, in 2007.

3 Edward Said, 'Bases for Coexistence', in *The End of the Peace Process*: *Oslo and After* (New York: Pantheon Books, 2000), p. 207. The essay was originally published in *Al-Hayat*, 5 November 1997.

4   Mikkel Borch-Jakobsen, 'The Freudian Subject, from
    Politics to Ethics' (Richard Miller and X. P. Callahan
    trans.), in Rosalind E. Krauss, Annette Michelson, Yve-
    Alain Bois, Benjamin H. D. Buchloh, Hal Foster, Denis
    Hollier and Silvia Kolbowski (eds), *October: The Second
    Decade, 1986–1996* (Cambridge, MA: The MIT Press,
    1998; October Books Series), pp. 329–74. Originally
    delivered as a lecture in June 1986 as part of the semi-
    nar 'The Subject in Psychoanalysis' at the Psychoanalytic
    Institute, Paris.

5   Martha Nussbaum, 'Rape and Murder in Gujarat:
    Violence against Muslim Women in the Struggle for
    Hindu Supremacy', in Amrita Basu and Srirupa Roy
    (eds), *Violence and Democracy in India* (London/New
    York/Calcutta: Seagull Books, 2007), pp. 101–22.

6   Christopher Bollas, 'The Structure of Evil', in *Cracking
    Up: The Work of Unconscious Experience* (London:
    Routledge, 1995), pp. 180–256.

7   'To get on familiar terms with the local people is a part
    of your education. To know only agriculture is not
    enough; you must know America too. Of course if, in
    the process of knowing America, one begins to lose
    one's identity and falls into the trap of becoming an
    Americanised person contemptuous of everything
    Indian, it is preferable to stay in a locked room.'—
    Rabindranath Tagore, 1907, in a letter to his son-in-
    law Nagendranath Gangulee, who went to America to
    study agriculture. Quoted in Amartya Sen, 'Tagore and
    His India', in *The Argumentative Indian: Writings on*

Indian History, Culture and Identity (New York: Farrar, Straus and Giroux, 2005), p. 105. The Isaiah Berlin quote about Tagore cited by Sen in the same essay ('Isaiah Berlin summarizes well Tagore's complex position on Indian nationalism') reads as follows: 'Tagore stood fast on the narrow causeway, and did not betray his vision of the difficult truth. He condemned romantic overattachment to the past, what he called the tying of India to the past "like a sacrificial goat tethered to a post", and he accused men who displayed it—they seemed to him reactionary—of not knowing what true political freedom was, pointing out that it is from English thinkers and English books that the very notion of political liberty was derived. But against cosmopolitanism he maintained that the English stood on their own feet, and so must Indians. In 1917 he once more denounced the danger of "leaving everything to the unalterable will of the Master", be he brahmin or Englishman.'—Isaiah Berlin, 'Rabindranath Tagore and the Consciousness of Nationality', in *The Sense of Reality: Studies in Ideas and Their History* (New York: Farrar, Straus and Giroux, 1997), p. 265.

8   Brinda Bose and Subhabrata Bhattacharyya (eds), *The Phobic and The Erotic: The Politics of Sexualities in Contemporary India* (London/New York/Calcutta: Seagull Books, 2007).

9   *Paradise Now*, directed by Hany Abu-Assad, 2005.

10 See Ze'ev Jabotinsky, *Samson the Nazarite* (London: M. Secker, 1930).

11 One of two essays published in *Reflections on War and Death* (A. A. Brill and Alfred B. Kuttner trans.) (New York: Moffat, Yard & Company, 1918).

12 'Partition, Proust and Palestine', the first P. K. Ghosh Memorial Lecture organized by the Seagull Foundation for the Arts, Kala Kunj, Calcutta, 5 January 2008.

13 In Eyal Ben-Ari and Yoram Bilu (eds), *Grasping Land: Space and Place in Contemporary Israeli Discourse and Experience* (New York: State University of New York Press, 1997; SUNY series in Anthropology and Judaic Studies), pp. 203–16.

14 'Nadine Gordimer to Ruth Weiss, 27 June 1979', in Ronald Suresh Roberts, *No Cold Kitchen: A Biography of Nadine Gordimer* (Johannesburg: STE, 2005), p. 369.